HELPING
OTHERS IN
• CRISIS •

MONEY PROBLEMS

RICHARD D. PERRY

KV-364-462

David C. Cook Publishing Co.
Elgin, Illinois—Weston, Ontario

Thank You
Thank you, Hope, for being my quiet and gentle strength and a great example of how to spend money wisely.

David C. Cook Publishing Co.
Elgin, Illinois/Weston, Ontario
Money Problems
© 1987 David C. Cook Publishing Co.

Scripture quotations, unless otherwise noted, are from the Holy Bible: New International Version. © 1973, 1978, 1984 by the New York International Bible Society. Used by permission of Zondervan Bible Publishers.

Published by David C. Cook Publishing Co.
850 N. Grove, Elgin, IL 60120
Cable Address: DCCOOK
Designed by Christopher Patchel
Photo by Bakstad Photographics
Illustrated by Jane Sterrett

Printed in the United States of America
Library of Congress Catalog Card Number: 86-73209

ISBN: 1-55513-797-0

CONTENTS

A RE YOU PREPARED TO HELP PEOPLE IN FINANCIAL HARD-
ship, in financial crisis?
As a Christian leader, you need to be aware of the
spiritual and emotional reasons people have problems with money. And after you are aware, you need practical ways to help
them. This is the focus of this book.

I faced my first financial crisis when I was 12 and a student at
a missionary kids' school. I'd been at the school since I was six
years old. My parents were far away—ministering in another
country—and I was very much alone.

I needed friends, and when I looked around at my peers, I
discovered the primary ingredient to friendship was money. I
observed that kids with money, clothes, American candy, and
records seemed to have friends. Money bought these things
which in turn bought friends, so money was my goal.

Being a missionary kid in those years meant doing without
licorice, bubble gum, American hot dogs, and those yummy,
chewy Milky Way candy bars—the four essentials of life. There
was also very little pocket change, at least when I compared my
bounty with those kids from the foreign embassy, United States
military, and government. So where was I going to get my
"friendship" money?

The student council store! I figured out how to steal handfuls
of money, and with it, I rose to the top of the popularity chart.

It took several months, but eventually I did get caught and
kicked out of school. I learned a couple of important lessons
from that experience. First, of course, stealing isn't worth it.
But, second, I began to understand that money can cover up a
problem, but it doesn't make it go away. Money has a way of
making people believe they don't have the needs they had before
they had money.

Money: Why do we want it so badly? Why do we spend it the
way we do? Why is it so difficult to control? These aren't just

questions for a lonely seventh-grade boy. They are questions we deal with in our own lives and in the lives of those people to whom we minister.

One summer during high school, I worked in a funeral home. One of my duties was to help the funeral home personnel at memorial services. I would greet those attending, help them to their seats, and be available after the service to assist the family in making the transition to the cemetery for burial.

I was shocked by many of the conversations I overheard. Money often played a bigger role than sorrow. I got early insights into the adult importance of money. Mothers and fathers arguing about money with children. Children with children. Aunts against uncles. Grandparents against grandchildren. Non-family members even joined in!

For a seventh grader, money had bought friends. Obviously, its value grew as people did. For adults, having control of money and property were far more important to many people than really loving those close to them.

Money! Learning to handle and use it in a Christlike way is not an option for a Christian. It's an imperative.

My job for most of the last 15 years has involved raising money for Christian ministries. Most of the $50 million raised through my efforts has come from individuals. Surely, those people had a right perspective on money, I assumed as I began this huge and worthwhile task. But as time went on, I realized that not all people who are giving to good causes are doing it for the right reasons. Some, like the lonely missionary kid I had been, were trying to buy friendship. Others searched for simple human contact. I remember one woman who lived alone and gave more times a month than seemed reasonable. We heard from her often—her letters and phone calls always filled with warmth and appreciation. She hardly ever talked about or was curious about the ministry she was giving the money to. She just wanted to communicate with someone. Her money bought love and companionship. How much better for her if she had realized that the best and most lasting love is not bought by giving money to others—or even to organizations that are doing the work of the Lord.

Money can be used as a club, a way to bat someone over his or her financial head. In my position as fund raiser, I saw this happen frequently. Parents or relatives would give money to a worthy cause and in the process let their kids know they were no longer valued.

I remember a couple in their sixties sitting in my office discussing how they should write their will. At the beginning of our meeting, I thought we were just going to finalize the details of how the ministry I worked for would benefit from their estate. Instead, the meeting turned into a heated debate on the merits of giving more to their children.

The mother argued that the six figures each child was getting wasn't enough. The father countered: "That's more money than the kids have earned. My money is meant for other things besides the children." And furthermore, he added, the child she was thinking of didn't deserve any more. "If there are going to be more arguments, keep in mind that you didn't earn this money in the first place."

The meeting went on for almost two hours while I quietly witnessed years of anger and resentment verbalized. It's true, money may not have been the root cause, but nothing else had as effectively brought up so many suppressed issues.

Money has caused disagreements, broken relationships, suspicion, division, and pain. It's no wonder that the Scriptures so strongly warn against the dangers of loving it. Christian leaders must be ready to handle this issue.

Let me briefly tell you how I will approach this subject in this book.

First, what you won't find. I am not a financial expert. So you won't find a lengthy discussion on how money came to be, how our economy works, and where the world is going economically.

Now, what you will find. The focus of this book will be spiritual and behavioral. We will look at the spiritual and emotional reasons people have problems with money. And we will discover how to help them.

Case studies will put you face-to-face with people facing the most typical money problems. Even though you don't know them, you'll recognize them in your network of family, church members, and acquaintances.

I'll introduce you to the National Foundation on Consumer Credit, Debtors Anonymous, SpenderMenders, Family Service America, and a host of other organizations you can recommend to anyone facing financial difficulties.

And we'll explore the Scriptures and review God's basic

principles for living. In the pages of God's Word, you'll discover how to help a friend or loved one burdened by debt or the urge to spend.

As you read this book you will encounter a recurring theme. People have problems with money for two basic reasons: They are victims of poor health, an accident, or unemployment; or because they have unmet emotional and spiritual needs.

Hopefully, the information I've compiled here, coupled with the truth of God's Word and your love, will be all you need to help meet those needs.

One further note: My special appreciation must be expressed to John Duckworth, who wrote Chapter 6 of this book, "Personal Financial Crisis and Your Whole Church."

CHAPTER ONE

PROBLEM DEFINITION: LIVING ON TOMORROW'S INCOME

A FAMILY'S HOUSE BURNS DOWN. THE CHURCH RALLIES TO help them, and within a short time almost everything is back to normal.

A child needs an expensive operation or he will die. The cost is way beyond the ability of the family. But the news gets around. Donations pour in, and the child is saved.

A congregation has outgrown the local school gym. The pastor presents a plan for buying property of their own, and within six months a ground breaking takes place.

A father has just abandoned his wife and three small children, leaving them with all the bills and obligations. The wife does not have enough money for food this week and one of the children has turned frightfully ill. An anonymous benefactor pays the bills and covers her child's doctor bill.

A famine sweeps over an African nation. Thousands are dying every day. But the world gives and the dying stops.

A child's bike has just been stolen and there are no words, explanations, or hugs that will make it better. But as soon as the news that mom and dad will buy her a new bike reaches her ears, the tears disappear and she hardly remembers that the bike had been stolen in the first place.

Money does so many wonderful things! Yet it becomes the cause of so much that's wrong in our lives.

Money problems can be caused by uncontrollable situations: accidents, poor health, the loss of a job. Sometimes, people just are not aware of the difference between the amount of income they have and their expenses. And it's not until a real crisis surfaces that they're educated to the role they can play in making the situation.

Most often, however, money problems are caused by the choices people make: They want more than they can afford. These wants are intensified by peer pressure and advertising. There are few cultures outside Western culture who face the tremendous pressure to be more by acquiring more.

In 1984, $88 billion[1] was spent on advertising in the United States alone. This amount rises each year. Advertising has only one purpose: to convince the target that he or she needs to purchase. The vast majority of advertisers have as their goal to increase their share of the market and increase sales. Where responsibility lies has been the subject of countless conversations. Is the advertiser responsible for the results of advertising? Or is the consumer responsible to act responsibly?

It used to be that advertising was general in its targeting. Advertisers took out newspaper and magazine ads or bought time on radio and television to reach a general audience.

As the media got more sophisticated so did the advertisers.

Consider this: WXYZ is the favorite television station of the John Viewpoint family. John likes the morning and evening news shows and documentaries. John's wife, Mary, loves the late morning and early afternoon soap operas. Bobby, their son, can't seem to stay away from the cartoons which strategically come on when Bobby wakes up and tend to fade when he goes to school. Susan, their daughter, tunes into the late afternoon hard rock music program. She joins her family in watching almost every police action program in the evening.

The television station has broken down all of these viewer segments and documented what types of people are watching each segment. Different advertising rates are given to each segment and sold to the advertiser wanting to reach that audience.

It makes sense. If you want to reach children, buy time during the children's programming. This is targeted advertising. Or targeted marketing.

In recent years the analysis and segmenting has gone another step. In 1983, the Director of the Stanford Research Institute's Values and Life-Styles Program, Dr. Arnold Mitchell, published the book *The Nine American Lifestyles, Who We Are and Where We Are Going*. In it is "a comprehensive look at the values, beliefs, drives, needs, and social trends that shape us and our lives."[2] The primary thesis of the book is stated up front: "More than anything else, we are what we believe, what we dream, what we value. For the most part we try to mold our lives to make our beliefs and dreams come true."[3]

The book, the result of years of research and analysis of Dr.

Mitchell and his colleagues, "analyzes and systematizes the values and lives of Americans today in such a way as to yield insights into why people believe and act the way they do."[4]

The conclusion: All Americans fall into the following nine groups of people.

Need-driven Groups:
1. The Survivor Life-Style
2. The Sustainer Life-Style

Outer-directed Groups:
3. The Belonger Life-Style
4. The Emulator Life-Style
5. The Achiever Life-Style

Inner-directed Groups:
6. The I-Am-Me Life-Style
7. The Experiential Life-Style
8. The Societally Conscious Life-Style

Combined Outer- and Inner-directed Group:
9. Integrated Life-Style

The largest group is the Outer-directed Group with 108 million American adults. The largest segment is The Belonger Life-Style with 57 million adults.

Along with interests and values, the activities and consumption patterns of each group have been documented. Further research has shown people holding the same values and consumption patterns tend to live and work together. This supports the cliché that "birds of a feather flock together." Analysts have looked at each zip code area of the country and correlated each one to a life-style type above.

The result is that marketers and advertisers can now target their message right down to the blocks around your house and the groups of people holding the same values!

You need to be aware of the relationship of advertising to the problems people have with money.

If an advertiser can figure out the emotional-psychological track of the target and what that person believes and values, the advertiser can make the message "be more by spending more" substantially more convincing.

Advertising is not wrong. It can play an important part in educating the consumer. But, too many times advertising convinces people that they will somehow become better, be more loved and accepted, achieve more, if only they buy a certain product or maintain a particular life-style.

Add to advertising's sophistication the fact that lenders have become more aggressive than ever before. Never has it been so easy to borrow money. The baby boom generation has a higher expected lifetime earning potential, and the lenders are willing to lend against it.

In one six-month period in 1985, installment loans increased 20 percent and now amount to more than $612.3 billion which is 22.4 percent of all after tax income. That means that when Mr. or Ms. Average American gets a paycheck, before the earner can do anything else, he or she must put 22.4 percent into installment loans. This does not include home mortgages![5]

But it gets worse! Total household debt has now risen to an almost unbearable 81 percent of the after-tax income, and savings have dropped from a postwar average of 6.6 percent after tax income to a record low of 1.9 percent![6] This means we are saving substantially less and obligating ourselves more. There used to be a greater margin for error. Now if a family can't pay, there aren't too many alternatives.

We now owe $11,318.60 for every man, woman, and child in America! Everyone![7]

And according to the analysts it's not going to get better. As a nation, and this is just counting consumer debt, we are going into debt at a rate of $35.2 billion every year![8]

Looking at it from a national perspective, Americans owe someone else $5 trillion dollars. Our society has slowly evolved into a people that live today on tomorrow's income.

What does all this borrowing mean out in the marketplace where you and I live?

1. According to the National Foundation for Consumer Credit, a nonprofit group that helps people with their financial problems in over 250 offices nationwide, the number of people coming to them for assistance is up 15 percent.[9]

2. Delinquent customer loans are now at $11.6 billion.[10]

3. 5.66 percent of all home mortgages, the type of loan people pay most promptly, are one month overdue.[11]

4. Hundreds of thousands of people are on the edge of bankruptcy. In 1984 alone 344,275 individuals declared bankruptcy; 578,000 more filed.[12]

If you place all of these statistics into a broader context a more alarming picture develops. Our money is worth less today. You must earn $3.00 today for what $1.00 bought in 1960. In 1945, 50 active workers supported one person on Social Security. In 1985 there were 3.3 people working for every person on Social Security. By the year 2030 only two people will support one person on Social Security. All of this while more than 26.7 percent of all households in the United States had no income in 1984 from wages, salary, or self-employment![13]

More and more people are in trouble because they are spending and borrowing too much. They're living, wanting, and buying beyond what they can personally support. And unless someone helps them, they will go through a tremendous amount of pain and personal crisis.

Outside factors are not the only influence on spending. There are inward ones as well. Psychologists and social scientists tell us that more and more, people feel unloved. So people must spend to compensate for a poor self-image. We'll explore this subject in depth later.

Another factor in uncontrolled spending is the departure of Christians from basic Biblical values. We and our nation in general are self-oriented and preoccupied with our own financial security.

In the Christian community, the so-called "theology of prosperity" (the belief that if you become a Christian countless blessings in the form of financial and material rewards will automatically fall into your life) has made its contribution to this problem. Those who hold this view try to make prosperity happen at a faster rate by spending and going into debt.

There are many reasons why people have problems with money. But in my judgment all money problems fall into four major categories:

1. The person is the victim of an uncontrollable situation such as an accident, the loss of a job, a loss of health, an event that caused emotional trauma, etc.

2. The person has a poor self-image and must find a way to "make" himself or herself better.

3. The person is not a Christian and is pursuing humanistic, self-oriented, and destructive values. Or if the person is a Christian, the person has moved away (directionally) from Biblical values and has become susceptible to those of the world.

4. The person holds to some theology or belief that personal prosperity, wealth, and an abundance of material possessions are mystically foreordained and therefore rightfully his or hers.

In counseling people with financial problems, it is important to determine what the origin of the problem is. Then, as you are treating the symptoms, namely stopping the spending and figuring out how to pay the bills, you can begin to go deeper into what caused the problem in the first place. Only then can you make sure that it won't happen again.

Most of this chapter has been given to defining the problems people have with money and what the major causes are. Before moving on, consider this list of symptoms—ways that you can tell if a person is in trouble financially. Individual symptoms may not be hard-and-fast proof that a problem with money is just around the corner, but they are clues.

Being unemployed. This is the most obvious clue, but I've placed it here because many people feel a need to spend more when they are unemployed. The good feelings that come with a purchase are coupled with a belief that things purchased on credit really don't have to be paid back, at least not very soon.

Collecting bills. Paying bills on time is not an ideal. It is a must. If they are overdue the person is headed into trouble. (Many times people will take an option not given them by the creditor. They will pay bills on a 45-to-60-day basis. They take the option, hoping that no one will notice.)

Going into savings to pay bills. The purpose of savings is to put away money for a future event and to have a buffer in times of emergency. This implies that one does not dip into savings unless the preplanned event arrives or there is an emergency or cash flow problem. A key symptom of a problem is a trend to rely on savings every month to pay bills.

Borrowing money from one account to pay another. We've all done it at one time or another, but to rely on the money put away for insurance premiums to help pay off the credit card is playing with disaster.

Operating close to the limit on credit cards. This means the person is not only within sight of how much the card company will allow him or her to spend, but also that the person cannot pay the card off and can barely pay the minimum required.

Having credit cards canceled.

Putting off going to the dentist or doctor. Because the money is so tight, taking care of one's health is now not important. In fact, it is impossible. Some people believe health is one asset that can bear a lot more pressure and burden than many other things in life.

Delaying payments of the essentials of life. This means putting off paying the utility bill, even in the middle of winter, or not paying insurance or doctor's bills.

Making minimum payments on loans. Some might think this is the norm, but a good money manager tries to pay off loans as soon as possible unless there is a tax advantage in not doing so.

Taking out new loans as soon as old ones are paid off. This does not mean taking out new loans is bad. It means that there is almost an urgency to buy something else now that the money is available.

Borrowing money from friends and family. It's not a good idea in the first place, and it can be the first sign that things are not going well.

Having difficulty in saving money.

Lying about financial situation. If not outright lying, then having difficulty admitting there is a problem. When confronted or asked if something is wrong, the person says that everything is fine or puts the problem in the past: "Oh, I used to have a problem, but everything is under control now."

Using one overdraft account to cover another. This is dishonest and against the law, but some people really believe they have the money in at least one of the accounts.

Having monthly installment loan payments that exceed 20 percent of take-home pay. This does not include the home mortgage payment. Another way to look at this is that total household debt exceeds 33 percent of annual discretionary income. If payments exceed this limit the person involved is living dangerously.

CHAPTER TWO

CASE STUDIES:
PEOPLE AND MONEY

THE PEOPLE IN THE FOLLOWING CASE STUDIES ARE NO DIFFER-
ent from you or me, no better or worse. But they either
have difficulty controlling money, controlling the urge to
spend, or are victims of circumstances beyond their control.

The cases you will read here are composites of situations from
life. The names are fictitious. The intent here is to illustrate the
types of problems people have so that when you encounter these
same situations in your network of friends and acquaintances
you'll be able to recognize them and, with God's help, begin to
make a difference in their lives.

The Emulators

Situation: Peter was born on the farm near a small mid-
western town. Things were tough in those days and early in his
high school years he decided not to be stuck on the farm the way
his parents were. So he set his goals high and, much to the
dismay of his parents, decided to go into marketing.

In college he met and married Mary. She was an ambitious
woman with her eye on a lucrative career in advertising. She had
come from a broken home and was determined to make her life
count. Both were Christians.

Mary landed a job in a small public relations firm and Peter
found a job in sales at a local radio station. They had a combined
income of over $45,000, more money than they had ever
dreamed of making just a few years before!

They bought a house, another car, signed up for all the major
credit cards, and began spending like they had never done
before. For the first year they controlled the spending, but as
their circle of friends became more intimate, they started comparing what they earned and had acquired to what their friends
had acquired.

In fact, many conversations at social gatherings surrounded
the latest financial opportunity and the most recent and trendiest

17

acquisition. Mary recalls that after each of those parties when she and Peter were on the way home, they would talk about how much they wished they were like the rest of their friends, and how nice it would be to own the product or article of clothing one of their friends had just told them about.

Usually the heavy buying would occur on the weekend following such a party, although one week they impulsively went out and traded in their old car for a trendy import.

The pattern of spending continued and imperceptibly increased. When the credit card bills arrived, Mary started by paying them off completely. But as the months rolled by, it became more important to have that cash for immediate things. It wasn't long before just the minimums on the credit cards were paid.

The turning point came one night when Peter and Mary were reviewing their financial situation. Mary wanted to pay the minimum on the MasterCard and Visa bills but Peter insisted they reserve the cash for that stereo system they'd been looking at. They let the payments slide and from that point on they never caught up again, not only with their credit cards but also with the car payments, one personal loan, and the house payment.

During the following year they lost their home, and one car. They had a portion of their wages assigned to debt retirement, and almost lost their marriage.

Insights: Peter and Mary began measuring themselves against what others did and had. What started innocently became compulsive. Soon that measure dominated their lives and drove them to spend—to be more by buying more.

The Divorced Buyer

Situation: Bill had just gone through an ugly divorce. His wife had left him for another man, claiming that he was not a good provider, companion, or friend. The process, which lasted six months, was devastating.

Bill and his former wife had three children, two boys and a girl. One weekend when he had the kids, he overheard them arguing. His daughter was defending him against the allegations of one of the boys. He was restating what their mother had told them: all of Bill's shortcomings and her opinion that he was also physically ugly.

Bill tried to put the comments down as child's play, but they reached his heart and hurt. He was slightly overweight. He was convinced that his looks were the major reason why women were not attracted to him, why he was alone. He felt clumsy, ugly, and useless.

He began to take people at the office out to lunch and dinner, always using his credit card to charge it. He'd ask friends to come over on the weekend, buy them a meal, take them to a special event like a game, and pay for it all. He would buy expensive gifts and books and give them to friends and acquaintances.

When his kids came over for a weekend, he'd spend a good portion of his paycheck on them. Clothes, toys, the circus, and lots of eating out was a regular routine.

But inside he still felt alone and unloved. And when the bank called about two overdraft checks his sense of alienation increased. Even the bank didn't love him! Bill was in trouble financially.

Insights: During his divorce and after it Bill should have gone to his pastor or a Christian friend who could help him deal with his feelings of inadequacy. Instead Bill chose to buy friendship and companionship. He was even trying to buy his children's affection. He spent money to buy love almost to the point of financial ruin. Had he known that he was worth a lot, that he was loved by God, other Christians, and his children, he may have avoided the problems with money. Bill could have been encouraged to join a small group at his church and to develop relationships with other divorced persons. Together they could have worked through their feelings.

Church Shyster

Situation: Joseph showed up in church on Sunday morning wearing tattered but clean clothes. His obvious poverty was in striking contrast to the rest of the congregation who were dressed in their Sunday best.

The pastor spoke to Joseph after the service and got bits of his story. "Lost my job and family. Just sort of wandered around and found this church. No money. You're such nice people."

The pastor invited him home to lunch, found him a warmer coat, gave him ten dollars, and suggested several places Joseph could apply for a job.

The next Sunday Joseph was back. "No job," he said. "I

tried, but no one wants a bum like me.''

The next Sundays followed the same pattern. Someone in the church would feed Joseph, often give him articles of clothing, and send him on his way with ideas for job hunting and money to help him until he got the job.

When one of the men felt Joseph was taking a little long to get on his feet, he checked the two businesses he had suggested. Joseph had been to neither. As people compared notes, they realized Joseph had been playing on their guilt, using them. The Sunday they expressed their feelings to Joseph, he thanked them for what they had done for him and left the church. He did not return.

Insights: Wise church leaders, especially in urban areas, will have thought through how to help people like Joseph. People do misuse the church—taking from it resources, time, and emotional energy. How do Christians separate the genuinely needy from the con artists?

One church set aside a fund and used the money to help people who wandered into the church. A Christian was assigned to the visitor and everything was done to walk the person through the process of getting a job and making life changes. If the visitor was not cooperative, the helper made certain the visitor knew he or she was always welcome in the church—to worship and make friends. But the visitor was not going to be given resources that were for the genuinely needy. More about this in Chapter 6.

Losing a Job

Situation: For years Andy had been the proud supporter of his family. As a kid he had been taught that hard work was important. He had also learned that the man of the house was the provider and that a man's wife should stay at home. He came from a conservative church background where he was taught to love God, his country, and his family. Andy was a strong man with deep convictions.

Jane came from a wealthy family in the city. She did not have a church background. In her senior year in high school a friend led her into a personal relationship with Jesus Christ. She began going to the same church Andy went to and soon adopted the spiritual and social values it taught.

Andy and Jane found each other at that church, fell in love, and married. They stayed in the same city because Andy had a good job in the steel industry—a job he had had for six years.

Life for Andy and Jane took a turn for the worse the day Andy lost his job. Andy came home broken and hurt but filled with the conviction that God would take care of him. They had saved some money and with the severance check Andy figured he could take up to six weeks to find a new job.

He began looking the next day. But everywhere he looked, Andy received the same answer: "The imports are hurting us; they can do it so much cheaper." Andy was determined to prove them wrong. He would find, any day now, a job that used his abilities.

About the fifth week Andy and Jane sat down to talk through their plan for the next two weeks. Money was running low and still there was not any prospect for a job. Jane suggested she get a job to buy them more time. Andy quickly rejected the idea, stating it was his duty and responsibility to support the family.

Andy's solution was to borrow the money he needed to buy more time. He borrowed money from a friend on the promise that he would pay it back in a month. His father also lent him some money. And he used his credit card for small purchases like gas for the car.

Another month passed before Andy realized he needed help. By then he had managed to spend all their savings, borrow $3000 from family and friends, and run his credit card up to $800.

Insights: Although they didn't know it at the time of their marriage, Andy and Jane held substantially different views on who should work and when. This area is often overlooked in premarital counseling. More time is spent on matters related to loving and serving each other, sex, and children, than on money and work.

Andy and Jane could have profited by a discussion on this subject. They may have uncovered how strongly Andy felt about his wife not working.

A Christian helper might have convinced Andy that Jane's working until he found a good job would not violate his beliefs. Jane had very marketable skills . . . skills that could have brought enough cash into their home to prevent them from borrowing.

Secondly, once he knew that he was not going to land the ideal job very soon, Andy should have taken any job to assure that cash was coming into the household. Pride and a belief that something good is just around the corner have a way of preventing one from being practical.

Andy should never have borrowed money from a friend or from his father. He placed those relationships in jeopardy.

While it is true that relatives and friends will usually give a person more time to pay back a debt, it's also true they feel a lot more strongly about the passing of time than a bank. A bank just *states* that the person is overdue and recovers the property. A relative *thinks* about how much time has passed and develops increasingly intense feelings about the person who has borrowed the money.

Prosperity Theology

Situation: Randy and Pat began attending a suburban church, and almost immediately they noticed the contrast between their struggling life-style and that of many of the young couples around them. When they mentioned it, a friend said that his success was due to his close walk with God. "If a person does what God wants, God will make him healthy, wealthy, and successful." Many people had a high orientation toward earning money. Both spouses worked. There was a sense that everyone had to make financial and material dreams come true.

Over and over, Randy and Pat heard people say, "One of God's higher purposes for Christians is to make them prosperous financially and materially." And for everyone else, the formula seemed to be working.

Finally the pressure caused by comparison became too much. They began to borrow heavily to create equity between how they were doing and how everyone else seemed to be doing.

Insights: Randy and Pat sincerely wanted to live for God but were unaware of how much that desire, coupled with their friends' prosperity theology and a need to be seen as receivers of God's blessing, caused them to become financially irresponsible.

A wise spiritual advisor could have helped Randy and Pat examine the life philosophies of their yuppie friends. They needed to separate the prosperity that can often come from hard work from the absolute assertion that prosperity is God's blessing. Money and things can often pull people away from God, bringing leanness to their souls. The couple was allowing others to define what God's Word taught instead of following the

Bereans' example in Scripture—to search the Bible for themselves to find out what things are true.

Never, Never Enough

Situation: Rhoda and her baby son were still living at a Salvation Army shelter when she started coming to church. Everyone rallied around her supplying love, food, money, a place to live, child care while she looked for a job. Rhoda's story was awful, so filled with hurt that the church members doubled their efforts to help her heal. She had become pregnant by another man and her husband had thrown her out. She had no money and no friends who would take her in. She went from southern belle to bag lady in a few months.

With church members' help, her life began to improve—a new job, enough money to support herself. But no sooner was she almost on her feet than she lost the job. This became a repeated pattern: job, light at the end of the tunnel, lost job, despair.

Rhoda would spend hours and hours going over her story with friends at the church. Then for practically no reason she would blow up at them and announce, "I refuse to be patronized by you. I don't need your help anymore." But of course she did.

Nothing seemed to help, not even the counseling that the church paid for. It was as if Rhoda had a great hole in her life. People could pour in friendship and love—pour and pour and pour, but it would all just dribble out the hole.

Insights: What better way to demonstrate Church than to provide a hospice for hurting, perhaps permanently damaged people? If people choose to participate in this Christian service, they need to be surrounded by a caring, praying support group. They will need spiritual refreshment, time away from the emotional struggles of people like Rhoda.

In Rhoda's case, the church provided money—for years and years until Rhoda herself got angry at the whole church and moved out of the state. But money was the least of the services offered. Very seldom, if ever, are the problems of hurting people solved exclusively with money. A trained core group of people, headed by or in touch with professionally trained people, needs to be one of the services offered by many churches. It is perhaps the most difficult assignment people can take on—to be a help and mentor to the poor, powerless, and oppressed.

Unaware

Situation: Ralph and Jan had been married almost three years before they realized they were in trouble. Both had come from very simple and unassuming backgrounds. Ralph's parents were from the inner city. Growing up had been tough. Ralph didn't remember any time when his dad had a steady job for more than a year.

Jan was from the same area. She had never had to deal with taking care of money, primarily because she didn't have much. As a child, basic needs were always taken care of.

Because both Ralph and Jan had decided to do more in life than their parents, they had made a special effort to develop their skills through junior college and special training. Ralph had become an outstanding auto mechanic, and Jan had found a comfortable niche as a court reporter.

They were pleased with their income, until to their surprise they discovered that they did not have enough money to cover all the bills. They never spent more than they had, so what was wrong? At first it was only one or two bills that were paid late. But progressively more and more were overdue.

Insight: Ralph and Jan were not impulsive and irresponsible spenders. They had problems because they had not set up a family budget and stuck to it. They were simply unaware that there was a difference between what came in and what went out. But because there was a lag between income and expense, that difference did not show up immediately.

Irregular payments such as life, health, and property insurance, annual car fees, taxes, maintenance of equipment are items that are easily forgotten in a budget. Ralph and Jan, for the most part, had correctly calculated the ongoing routine bills—bills that came every month. They had not reserved some of their weekly income for irregular payments.

Because they did not keep track of where they spent their money, certain spending patterns became more frequent, especially during those times when the amount of money on hand was greater than the bills currently in their apartment waiting to be paid.

For specific help on home budgeting see Chapter 4.

The Giver

Situation: Madeline had worked hard all her life as a factory worker. She, better than most people, knew how tough life was. Although she personally had not suffered much, she had seen plenty of people, some of them friends and family, go through very difficult times. She was now 73, retired, living alone, and on a pension.

The pension, coupled with her social security amounted to a meager $1100 a month—not much for a lady that had only missed six days of work in 46 years of continuous service. And that amount of money barely covered the small apartment she lived in, plus food and utilities.

Madeline was by nature a caring person. She was thankful that God had been so good to her. He had given her good health and protected her from any harm for so many years. She was often saying, "I owe God and others a lot because things have gone so well for me."

Financial problems for Madeline began when she started responding to appeals for money in her mail, on television, over the telephone, and at her door. It was difficult for Madeline to say no. The needs were so real and she cared so much. The more frequently she gave the more they called on her to give.

Of particular difficulty to Madeline was the request to make a pledge. It was easier for her to handle a one-time gift request. She would simply look in her purse or checking account and if she had it she would give. But pledges were a different matter.

And the letters in the mail were so urgent. So many people needed her help. And when she gave she'd receive such warm and loving letters back, thanking her for her concern and her financial help. As the months passed, the amount of fund-raising mail in Madeline's apartment grew. Madeline tried to respond to as many of the requests as she could. She was to the point where she was dipping into her grocery and health-care money to help others.

Madeline's soft and tender heart had pushed her to the edge of financial disaster.

Insight: At the center of Madeline's giving was her gratitude to God for having blessed and protected her for so many years. She was genuinely thankful and wanted to express her thankfulness by helping others. She was also lonely and therefore prone to creating relationships with people through the mail. In many ways she had an extended family in all of the people she gave money to. Her desire to help others coupled with her loneliness provided fertile ground for unhealthy relationships to develop.

The organizations involved were not unscrupulous or manipulative. There is no way they could have known Madeline's circumstances. Madeline was victimized by her own needs.

By revealing her problem to someone else, Madeline could have been helped to understand that she did not need to respond to every request, that the needs expressed would have been met by others, that it all did not depend on her.

Out of Work

Situation: John was out of work, again. Because he came from a very poor family that could not afford to even pay for transportation to a nearby trade school, John had been labeled as unskilled labor. He was 24, single, and on welfare.

He didn't want to be on welfare. In fact, as a Christian, John held to the belief that work was honorable and good. But he couldn't find a steady job within walking distance of the inner-city neighborhood where he lived with his parents. The competition for unskilled labor jobs was stiff. There seemed to be an overabundance of young people just like him always out looking. He could find temporary jobs, and he always took them. But finding a long-term job had so far been impossible.

Whatever money he did receive he gave to his parents, not only to help them out but in return for their giving him food and shelter.

The way John figured it, the only way to get ahead was to dress a little sharper, so that when he did go for an interview he would be more acceptable to the prospective employer. But because he didn't have any money to buy clothes, he borrowed some from a friend and bought what he needed.

John's first attempt at finding a job with his new look was emotional disaster. He walked in proud and confident only to be asked what he knew how to do. When the prospective employer discovered that John did not have the skills or experience necessary for his job, the interview ended courteously but abruptly. This situation was repeated several times before John realized that this attempt to dress up the outside had not helped him find the long-term job he wanted. Now he was in debt to a friend with no way to pay him back.

Insight: Give a person a fish, and you'll take care of today's hunger, but teach a person to fish, and he'll never go hungry again. In some cases, church members must get involved in training programs that will give people—not a handout—but a vocation that will last a lifetime.

One church in a depressed community set up an evening school. Members with skills taught classes, and people who were interested in training for a job signed up. The instructors donated their time, in electrical work, secretarial skills, operation of road equipment, hospital-aide skills. Students were required to pay a small amount to give them ownership in the course and to sign a paper promising to be at all classes.

Some church members may be willing, or work for companies that would be willing, to give an untrained person a reduced pay while he or she learns the job. Others may give training in exchange for free labor during the unemployed person's down time.

During training periods, it's wise to assign a Christian partner to meet regularly, perhaps daily at the beginning, with the untrained worker. Often people who have been out of work for a long time or who have never worked steadily, need regular encouragement and help in areas of skill development and people interaction. Many have poor work habits or attitudes toward authority that, if not corrected, will lead to their losing of the new job.

Perhaps you've never been unemployed or had problems with money. But millions of Americans—millions of Christians—do. And, as you've seen in the stories in this chapter, money is just the symptom of something deeper. Once you understand the details of the symptom, always look deeper for the core problem. Most of the time there is one. It will require your patience, understanding, and love to deal with it.

CHAPTER THREE

QUESTIONS AND ANSWERS

T HE GOAL OF THIS CHAPTER IS TO LIST THE MOST COMMON questions people ask about money. These comments will help you give structure to your own ideas. The intent here is not to supply word-for-word answers, but to point you in a direction so that you can flesh out the answers on your own.

Not all of the questions and answers in this chapter will be directly related to problems or crisis situations. I've included others because I believe people often get into problems because they don't know how to manage money. For instance, budgeting seems to be a very straightforward and noncrisis activity—so why include it in a book on crisis? Think of it this way. A person without a budget is headed for a crisis. After you've identified the problem people are facing, you'll have additional resources to get them on their feet in the area of money management.

Two recurring themes throughout this chapter will be discipline and control. People must learn to control the inner drive to spend and be disciplined about how they manage their money. I Corinthians 9:24-27 speaks to this attitude in life.

Do you not know that in a race all the runners run, but only one gets the prize? Run in such a way as to get the prize. Everyone who competes in the games goes into strict training. They do it to get a crown that will not last; but we do it to get a crown that will last forever. Therefore I do not run like a man running aimlessly; I do not fight like a man beating the air. No, I beat my body and make it my slave so that after I have preached to others, I myself will not be disqualified.

In order to win at the important things in life we must exercise self-control. Our minds and hearts should work for us, not drive us to fleshly, perishable ends.

For additional insights to money and the disciplined Christian life look into Richard Foster's book, *Money, Sex, and Power* (Harper and Row, 1985).

I've just lost my job. What do I do about my bills?

It's not easy to feel good about yourself when someone else, for whatever reason, has told you you're not needed anymore. Start working right away on your feelings about yourself. Don't let the little voices inside convince you that you're worthless, that you deserve not to have a job.

Ask God to help you value yourself, even now during this moment of crisis. Honestly evaluate why you lost the job.

Now to the bills. First, stop spending! This will be harder than you think. When a person goes through a crisis or experiences something that is emotionally disturbing, the tendency is to spend money to feel better. That's why you need to work on your feelings first. Then you'll have a better defense against spending. Remember, spending isn't going to do a thing for you.

Second, sit down and make a complete list of all your debts. Include those last credit card purchases. Everything. Total them up. This is the figure you have to get rid of before you decide to purchase anything else.

Create a plan to pay your debts. Divide the least forgiving debtors from the most forgiving. A car payment would be in the first group. A debt to a friend or relative might be in the latter. Although, remember, in not paying the first you may just lose a car, while in not paying the second you may lose a relationship.

The next step is to determine how you will pay off these debts. If you're getting severance pay from your employer, put some of it toward living expenses, the rest toward the most pressing debts. Don't pay them all off. The challenge is to buy time until you can get another job. So just pay off what you have to on the most pressing ones. If after applying this formula you find you have extra money, then pay off more.

It's easier to take care of the smaller bills, but I'm in deep trouble on my home mortgage. What should I do?

The first thing to do is visit the people who lent you the money. They are very interested in helping you keep current on your obligation to them. If they don't have an office in your community, they may have a toll-free number you can call. Before you call or visit you need to have some answers to the questions they will ask.

1. *How and why did you fall behind?* Be prepared to give all the details. Don't hold anything back. It's important to be honest and open with creditors from the beginning.

2. *What are your current sources of income?* They will want to know details of your income-producing activities, specifically if they are dependable and what the monthly amounts are. Be sure to include all sources of income, such as wages, union or disability benefits, welfare payments, VA benefits, Social Security, savings investments, spouse or children's income, etc.

3. *How do you plan to pay your mortgage?* This is your presentation on how you will use the income you've identified above to help you pay. You will have to share more of your personal life than you think. The lender needs to understand how you plan to spend all of your money so he or she can see where the mortgage payments fit into your budget. Remember, the lender wants to help.

Your lender may be able to work out a different repayment plan which could temporarily reduce or even suspend your monthly payments until you get back on your feet. If certain conditions apply, you can refinance your mortgage, or turn it over to HUD/FHA if it was insured by them. Or the lender may advise you to sell your home, and cut your losses.

There are some other people who can help. If your home loan was insured by the HUD/FHA or guaranteed by the Veterans Administration, contact their local office. They're in the phone book under U.S. Government Agencies. Call these offices only if your lender cannot help you any further. Sometimes there are local community or social organizations that can help you with credit counseling.

Family Service America maintains offices in 290 locations around the country. Call or write them for help:

Family Service America
11700 West Lake Park Drive
Park Place
Milwaukee, WI 53224

The local HUD office often has a list of HUD approved home ownership counseling agencies which may be able to help. Be aware of those in your church community. There may be someone in the church who is a financial counselor, banker, or attorney, who can give you advice.

(There are rip-off artists who will be more than happy to take your money and offer a solution to your problem. Especially watch out for people who will offer to speak to your lender on your behalf, stating that they have a high success rate at getting these kinds of problems solved. Your lender wants to talk to you, not someone else. And don't borrow money to make delinquent payments. Borrowing more money is never a solution.)

I am way over my head in debt with credit card and personal loan payments due, and yet I still borrow money.

Your situation has hardly anything to do with money and more to do with how you feel about yourself. You may be a compulsive spender. Compulsive spending is on the rise in the United States as more and more people try to find happiness in shopping and acquiring. But the results of such shopping sprees are anything but happy:

"I often leave the packages sealed for days, mustering up the courage to open them," said one woman from California. "I want to beat myself up. I scream, 'No more, I'll never overspend again,' only to repeat the shopping excursions a few days later."[1]

"Compulsive spending is rooted in a combination of psychological and social factors. The foremost causes are low self-esteem and feelings of powerlessness. 'For the shopping addict,' says Sandi Gostin of SpenderMenders, 'buying something gives a temporary illusion of control. Just by signing your name to a charge slip, you have the power to take home anything you want.' "[2]

How do you deal with this problem? "You have to start to attack the problem by interrupting either the trigger or the opportunity," says Dr. Carla Perez of San Francisco. "Resolving the emotional conflicts that cause addiction can take a very long time. But while you're working on the emotional trigger, you can take practical steps to interrupt the opportunity."[3]

One way to "interrupt the opportunity" is to make compulsive spending more difficult. Check your spending by waiting and not having "spending instruments" such as cash, checks, and credit cards on your person.

Other sources of help are organizations like SpenderMenders, P.O. Box 15000-156, San Francisco, CA 94115 or Debtors Anonymous, an organization for compulsive spenders modeled after Alcoholics Anonymous. Check your local telephone directory for a chapter in your area.

For counseling with a Christian perspective, check your telephone directory or seek recommendations from churches in your area.

I don't have a spending problem. But because of circumstances, I'm unable to pay my credit cards and loans. What should I do?

You need to contact the lender, explain your circumstances, tell your sources of income and your plan to repay what you owe. Then work out a plan you both can agree to. But be sure you talk to the lender. Most lenders are reasonable people, if they know you are serious about paying them back. But don't expect them to give you solutions that are free. Their solutions will cost you interest on the money you've borrowed.

I've just gone through a divorce, and I'm really scared about my finances. What should I pay attention to?

First of all get control of your feelings. This will take time. A divorce or separation is right next to death when it comes to the amount of stress it puts on a person. So work at gaining perspective about what has happened. Talk to friends, a counselor, and/or your pastor. Talk to God. Tell Him about your anger, your frustration and loneliness. He will help.

As you're doing this, create a budget. See Chapter 4 for specific instructions. The point here is that you are in a new situation. *You know* that income patterns will not be the same. But neither will the spending patterns. That means you need to recalculate everything. Go through the entire budget process. Just doing that will put you in touch with your financial reality and make you feel better because you are in control.

Don't put this off. The stress you are experiencing is partially caused by uncertainty. The sooner you work toward figuring out the details of your new life, the sooner you will be more at peace with what has happened.

I'm approaching bankruptcy and have a lot of fears about what people will think. Can you help?

More than 344,275 people went through bankruptcies in 1984 and 578,000 more filed.[4] As a Christian, you face some difficult choices in the days ahead.

You should avoid bankruptcy, if at all possible. There are several reasons for this: As a Christian, you have an obligation to repay money you have borrowed. Secondly, credit bureaus will keep your file for up to ten years after the bankruptcy which means that most lenders will not want to deal with you because of it.

If you decide to go ahead, here's what will happen. You will file and a judge will determine how your assets will be distributed to the people to whom you owe money. The actual filing fee will be under $100 although you may incur a lot more expense in attorney's fees to defend your case.

You should understand some basic things about bankruptcy. The purpose of bankruptcy laws is to give relief to the over-indebted family or individual. It should be used only in extreme cases of financial difficulty.

"Once a person is judged bankrupt by the court, all assets and possessions, except those exempted by federal and state law, are turned over to the court trustee to be sold. The proceeds are then distributed to creditors."[5]

There are two common types of bankruptcy for individuals: Chapter 7 in which all debt is cleared and Chapter 13 in which the person works out an arrangement with the court and the lenders to pay back debt.

Under Chapter 7 "a debtor can no longer exempt $200 of value on each item of household goods and clothes. There is now a flat $4000 maximum amount. In addition, a debtor can exempt only $3750 of equity in real property used as a residence plus $400 in value of other property."[6]

"Any debts of $500 for more for 'luxury goods and services,' owed to a single creditor and incurred within 40 days of filing, must be paid. So must cash advances of more than $1000 extended under an open-ended credit plan obtained by the debtor within 20 days before filing."[7]

By far the better route is Chapter 13, since it gives you relief while making sure you pay back what you owe. If you are considering bankruptcy as a solution to the problem you're currently in, consult either an attorney, or if you can't afford one, a Legal Aid or Legal Services office for more advice. You should know all the details before you proceed.

Concerning people's comments: There will always be people who will make judgments about you when you are in a difficult situation. You can't avoid it. The important thing is to make sure you're right about your relationship to your creditor. Are you committed to paying the creditor back? If you are, no one is justified in criticizing. You have fulfilled you moral and spiritual obligation.

Make sure you pay back what you owe and take steps to avoid

a similar situation in the future. These steps include, at the most basic level, creating and obeying a budget and curbing the impulse to spend.

How many credit cards should I have?

If you have to have any, then have only one—a major bank card. Choose either MasterCard or Visa, although you may have to pay an annual fee just for having the card.

Some stores are issuing cards that look like credit cards but aren't. All they do is establish that they can accept checks from you. If you have problems with overspending, the check cashing card will help you spend more. If you're in your favorite grocery or department store, just knowing that you can pull out that blank check and have it accepted without much trouble is a subtle license to spend.

You may want additional cards because it feels good to have so many. Or because having, using, and displaying them makes a statement to friends, relatives, and associates that you are successful. Examine these feelings. What do they say about you as a Christian?

How can I use credit cards wisely?

If you have to use the credit card, be sure you are in touch with the other bills that will hit your economy about the time the credit card bill will come in. Credit cards have a way of getting away from even the most disciplined person. And with all the messages in the media encouraging you to spend it's difficult to avoid doing so.

Another principle, given to me by David Mehlis, President of David C. Cook Publishing Co., is that if you have to use a credit card, don't use it for a consumable item. "If you can't see it when the bill comes due, don't charge it!" That means you shouldn't use a credit card for eating out, gas for the car, special outings, transportation, etc.

In summary:
- If you need to have a card, have only one.
- Charge only what you can pay off completely when the bill comes due.
- Pay all the bill—as soon as it is due.
- Charge only what you can see and touch when the bill is due.

35

Someone offers me a line of credit with no interest for a period of time. Should I take it?

Not necessarily. Many of those offers are to get you to buy, not to get you to pay. If the company making the offer can get you to accept its line of credit, it figures it's just a matter of time before you use it—and that's the ultimate goal: to help you buy. Once you've started a pattern of buying, you will probably continue that pattern in the future. And the company will charge you interest in the future.

Some things are impossible to buy without credit. How should I handle those?

That's true. For many people, it's impossible to buy a car and pay cash for it. In those situations, be sure you are getting a good interest rate and that you can handle the payments. Make the payment schedule as short as you can. Rather than take 48 months to pay it back, try to squeeze it into 24. The longer you take to pay back a loan the greater the risk that what you've bought will need to be replaced. Then you'll be paying twice.

If during the pay-back period you can pay the item off more quickly, do so. The idea is to get rid of debt. Remember, if you are borrowing within your means, the only purpose of credit is to advance time. You've been allowed, for a premium, to reach forward 12 to 48 months and borrow on your future earnings. Don't get out there too far.

It's healthy to be skeptical about your future earning potential. Don't cultivate paranoia that keeps you up at night. Instead, do not allow yourself to think that the future is merely an extension of the present, only better. If you think this way, you'll make a lot of decisions today you'll regret tomorrow. Be conservative.

Don't spend all of your paycheck. Put some of it into savings (see questions under savings and budgets) with a goal of spending it on major purchases. Have a car fund, an addition to your house fund, etc. Then all you have to do is reach into your savings and make that purchase.

What about borrowing from friends or relatives?

Don't do it! I know others do it and they don't have any problems. There's something about borrowing from people close to you that adds a false feeling of security and comfort to the borrowing procedure. It's easy to believe that if you get in trouble you can delay payment on this loan.

I've just paid off a loan and now I have extra cash. Isn't it safe to take out another loan?

No. Why not put the extra cash into savings? Why do you need another loan? Break the pattern and put the money into savings.

Is credit wrong?

Although credit itself is not wrong, what many people do to themselves because of it is. The Scripture suggests that we should "owe no man anything" and it does so for a purpose.

Do you want your life bound up by financial obligation?

If you are going to borrow, borrow money only for those things that retain some value. And only borrow an amount equal to the value of the property. That way, if you get in trouble, you can sell it and not owe anything. For instance, if you only put $300 down on a new car, the moment you drive it off the lot you will owe more than what you could sell the car for down the street. Make a big enough down payment on your purchases so that if you need to get out you can.

Will I prosper financially because I am a Christian?

God's highest priority with us is that we become like Him—not that we get rich. Take a look at I Timothy 6:6-8: "But godliness actually is a means of great gain, when accompanied by contentment. For we have brought nothing into the world, so we cannot take anything out of it either. And if we have food and covering, with these we shall be content" (NASB).

God is not obsessed with making us rich and prosperous. He'd rather we pursue other values. Now, because we are Christians, we should follow principles of integrity, honesty, and fairness in relationships. These coupled with wisdom may result in financial prosperity, but that is not our primary goal.

When considering our lives as Christians, remember:
1. God created all things and our relationship to them. We are to be good stewards of everything He has placed in our care. There is a proper use for all God has created.
2. Sin brings abuse (rather than proper use) to all God-given things. See I Corinthians 7:31; I Timothy 4:4, 5; 6:17b.
3. Our primary mission as Christians is to love God and serve Him.

As a Christian, what principles should I follow in the use of money?

I've covered some of them in this book already and I'll get into more detail later, but basically there are several major ones:
- Don't borrow if you can help it.
- Pay your bills on time. A Christian should never have to be reminded to pay up.
- Don't flaunt your wealth. If you've been blessed by God, be humble in the way you use your money.
- Spend wisely. Live within your means.
- Save money.
- Give generously to God's work and others. Use your money to do good.

I can't save money because my income just barely covers my living expenses. What should I do?

Most bills are not due on the very day you get your paycheck. Since that's true, leave only what you really need to spend until the next paycheck in your checking account. Put the rest in a savings account that allows unlimited deposits and withdrawals. Take money out only when you need to pay a bill.

Yes, it is a lot of trouble. But what you'll discover is that when you don't have easy access to your money, you will reduce expenses.

What kinds of things should I save money for?

If possible, you should always save money for a rainy day— the unexpected. This money is a cushion or security money. Every family has unplanned expenses. An appliance suddenly gives out; the car's brakes decide not to work; there's been a small accident and the deductible on insurance requires the family to pay the first $100.

You should also earmark a specific amount of money in each paycheck for bills that occur less often than once a month, or for special occasions—taxes on real estate, personal property, and income; schoolbooks and supplies; all types of insurance; vacations; medical checkups; Christmas.

Create a fund in savings for each of the major events. Then take a small amount out of each paycheck to build up the fund. You can't know how freeing it is when that bill comes in and you have the money to pay it without hurting your regular economy!

O.K. So you've told me what I should consider when I save money. What are some principles to follow in spending money?

Your question brings up the issue of needs versus wants. The question to ask every time you spend money is: Do I need it? If the honest answer is no, then don't buy it. We have been trained by advertising to believe that wants are needs.

Ask God to participate by helping you see through the advertising messages and to give you the strength to resist your wants. Let me suggest a prayer:

"Dear Lord, I'm starting the day again with You. You know how difficult it is for me to be like You. I want to, but there are also a lot of other things I want that aren't good for me. So, first of all, Lord, take those wants and help me get rid of them. And as I go out today, help me look at things the way You do—when I see or hear the advertisements, when I look at the displays in the stores, when I see my peers and friends and the things they have, help me not to want what I do not need. Help me understand during those specific times that what really matters is not what I have or what I can buy, but who I am. In Jesus' name, Amen."

Here's a pattern that, when followed, saves each of us from spending money foolishly.
- You see something you want.
- You ask yourself if you need it. If your answer is no, forget it.
- If you need it, delay. Wait until tomorrow.
- Talk to someone else about it. Pray about it.
- If everything still points to this being a wise purchase, and you can afford it, buy it.

God cares very much about how you spend your resources. And He wants to help you do it. Just ask.

Someone said I should have a will. Should I?

Yes, you should! You can't possibly know the grief some survivors go through when loved ones don't have one! First, a will is a way of protecting those left behind. In many states, if you haven't spelled out the distribution of your property, the state will. And your family will be the losers.

Second, those left behind may not know what you wanted to do with your property. By not spelling things out in advance, you leave a lot of questions unanswered that may result in deep divisions among your loved ones. Don't leave it up to them! You decide!

How do I make a will?

If you can afford it, go to an attorney. It's better to spend a little now and get the words right than to risk leaving something undefined. A simple will may cost about $100. Call a few reputable attorneys in your area and ask them how much they would charge. If you can't afford it, then at least make your wishes known in writing. Have a friend witness what you have written and have it notarized. If you feel comfortable with it, talk it over with a friend or spouse so someone knows your intentions. If you don't know what to write down, or how to write it, go to your library or a good bookstore and buy a book on the subject. The $10 to $15 you spend will be a bargain. There are several books I can recommend:

A Christian's Guide to Family Finances by Albert J. Johnson, Victor Books, 1983. Available at your local Christian bookstore.

Planning Retirement Income, Public Affairs Pamphlet No. 634. Available for $1 from Public Affairs Pamphlets, 381 Park Ave. South, New York, NY 10016.

The Retirement Money Book by Fred Nauheim, Acropolis Books Ltd., 1982. Available at your local bookstore or public library.

The important thing is to have thought through what will happen after you die. In addition to dealing with wills, these books deal with retirement planning. Read them. Plan for your future.

My spouse passed away without a will; I don't know what to do.

If your spouse had a lot of property, you may be in for some major problems. The first thing to do is get the advice of a Christian attorney or if you can't find one, a banker. Find someone who comes recommended. Widows and widowers are easy prey. Have someone else watching out for your affairs with you. Another source for help is the American Association for Retired Persons (AARP) at 1909 K Street, NW, Washington, DC 20049 or Family Service America at 11700 West Lake Park Drive, Park Place, Milwaukee, WI 53224. (414)359-2111.

How much should I give my kids for allowance?

Until they are old enough to baby-sit, deliver newspapers, or be involved in some kind of activity that pays, consider giving your child 10 to 15 cents times his or her age each week. That means if your child is eight years old the child would get 80 cents to $1.20 per week for allowance. The figure you choose will depend on your income.

Actually the amount you give per week is not as important as what you are teaching your child about money. Allowance should not be something you automatically give. That's not how paychecks work in real life. We have to earn them. So have some task around the house that when done through the week released the allowance into the child's hands. This work is symbolic in the early years.

Also be sure you teach your child the importance of giving to God. Pennies given with the right attitude on Sunday can teach the child that giving back to God is important.

How should I teach my children to value money and hard work?

It's not easy these days, but you can do it. If you model hard work and a value for money, your children will pick up your attitude. Talk about work in positive ways.

The best way for your child to learn about work and money is to see you enjoying work and learn from you that financial rewards are a result of work.

I can't seem to get a job, and when I do get one I don't have it very long.

The fact that you do get jobs means you can. You do know *how* to get a job! Why don't you keep them? Is it because you aren't skilled enough for the job? Ask your employer. By law he or she is obligated to give you a reason if you have been on the job six months or more. Listen carefully to his or her answer. Don't get angry. If you are underqualified, you need to get additional training.

You might not keep a job because you don't perform well. If that's the case, then you need to stop and think why. Make an honest list of the feelings you have at work. Do you feel tired? Lazy? Is it hard to work when no one notices how good a job you're doing? Do you get discouraged easily? If you're faced with a problem, do you give up? Are you afraid to tackle certain parts of the job? Are you afraid of people? Are you afraid of criticism? Does it make you angry?

Perhaps you're just not sure that the jobs you are in are the ones you want. Richard Bolles, author of *What Color Is Your*

Parachute? an excellent book that will help you figure out your skills and what to do with them, says: "You have got to know what it is you want, or someone is going to sell you a bill of goods somewhere along the line that can do irreparable damage to your self-esteem, your sense of worth, and your stewardship of the talents God gave you."[8]

Planning for your life's work is a major task that involves thinking, analyzing, and doing. You must "identify the core of your life, the constant thread, the constancy in you that persists through all the changing world around you."[9]

God has gifted you in a special way. You need to discover what that way is. Intercristo, a Christian career counseling service at 19303 Fremont Ave. North, Seattle, WA 98133 is an excellent source for help. Write them with confidence.

I can't even get a job, because I don't know how to do anything.

God didn't shut down when He was creating you. He has a definite purpose and plan for you. The challenge is to figure out what your gifts are and find a place they can be used. Here's how you can start on your journey.

First, work on the way you think and feel about yourself. Spend a lot of time in the Scriptures. Pray. Ask God to help you see what He sees in you. Ask Him to help you love yourself.

Next, make lists of the things you enjoy doing. You don't need to show them to anyone yet so write anything you feel—even if you think it's crazy. Another way to approach this is to think about what activities give you the most satisfaction. When do you feel the best? Spend some time on this list. I suggest writing something every night, even if you repeat yourself. Just write.

After a time of making lists, analyze what you have written. First, put all the like statements together. You're probably beginning to see a pattern emerge. You should have five to ten groups of statements.

Second, put next to each group the jobs you think are most related to the statements. For instance, if one of the groups looks like this, the jobs that follow might match them:

Group Your "I Enjoy" Statements
I like kids.
I like to explain things.
I feel good when I clean things.
I like to listen to people's problems.

Jobs Most Related

These statements might lead to being a teacher, a day-care center worker, or maybe a social worker or assistant in an agency that deals with kids.

To recap, the first goal is to figure out what situation you are most likely to be happy in. Notice I didn't say what job—just what situation. The next goal is to determine the type of job and this means analyzing what you do best. Your first list was made up of what feels best. Your second list was made up of jobs you might do best. For example, it could be that you're really organized, that every time you see a messy situation you tend to put it into some form. Maybe you are artistic. You seem to have a good feel for colors and form. It could be that you like using your strength. It feels good to lift heavy objects and work at physically difficult tasks. Or people usually say that you're the kind of person who is easy to talk to. You always have encouraging and wise words.

One thing you should notice is that you don't have to go to college to do any of those things well. It's not always a matter of education. God has gifted you with special abilities. Start believing it! The list of the things God helps you do especially well can go on for pages.

The Dictionary of Occupational Titles (produced by the U.S. Government Printing Office, Washington, DC 20402. Phone: (202)783-3238. This book should also be available at your local library.) breaks people's skills into three major areas: People, Data (or information), or Things. Richard Bolles uses this division to help people identify their skills. Which list sounds most like the skills you have identified?

PEOPLE[10]

Taking instruction
Serving
Communicating
Urging, Persuading, Selling
Amusing, Distracting, Diverting, Performing
Supervising, Managing
Instructing, Coaching, Teaching, Training
Consulting, Advising
Treating

Negotiating
Holistic, Counseling, Empowering, Mentoring

DATA[11]
Comparing
Computing
Compiling
Analyzing
Copying
Coordinating
Synthesizing, Innovating, Creating

THINGS[12]
Handling
Feeding, Loading, Emptying
Tending, Minding, Watching
Manipulating, Working (something)
Driving, Steering
Operating, Adjusting
Precision Working, Exhibiting One's Craft
Setting up, Restoring, Ensuring Effectiveness
Inventing

Your list should fall in a general way into one of the areas above. Once you have discovered which one, go to the *Dictionary of Occupational Titles*. Look up that area, and it will list types of jobs in that category. This is one way to get some general direction on what you like to do and what fits you best. It's not a replacement for good career counseling—but it will give you some ideas.

What we're trying to do is figure out what types of jobs might match what you enjoy doing and what you do well. Once you have these lists you still may not have the answer you're looking for. Don't worry. See if there is anyone in your church who is a successful business person. Perhaps the person would be willing to go over your list and give you advice.

If you have the money, add a job counselor to the list of people you get advice from.

CHAPTER FOUR

SETTING UP A BUDGET

P EOPLE WITH MONEY PROBLEMS SEEK HELP BECAUSE THEY want to live a more controlled, disciplined, secure life. One primary tool in achieving those goals is a budget. Many people don't have one because they just don't know how to set one up. Here's where you come in.

The following outline will guide you through the step-by-step process of setting up a budget. Use it to help others, augmenting it to fit each person's individual needs.

First, help the person understand what a budget is. It's simply a tool to help people spend their money wisely. There are several assumptions behind that statement:

• The person you are helping wants to spend money wisely.
• The person is willing to follow a plan with goals that determine how he or she will spend it.

The following pattern is developed as if you were talking personally to someone who has accepted the above assumptions.

Set Goals

After accepting the assumptions, the next step is to set goals. What does your family need and want for the future? The best way to determine this is to get together and talk about it. Don't leave the kids out! They have a lot to add to the conversation. Plus they'll learn some valuable lessons just watching you go through the process.

First, consider where you want to be 15 to 20 years from now. Next, where do you want to be in the next five years? And lastly, what do you want to accomplish in the next 12 months?

So you need three sets of goals: one for the long term, one for the intermediate, and one for the next year. Some examples of long-term goals might be: to have a debt-free home; educate our children; save for retirement. For the next five years: make a down payment on a home; buy a major appliance or a car; put that addition on. For this coming year: pay off all credit cards and outstanding loans; get a new desk; take that vacation; put a certain amount of money into savings as a cushion.

Goals do change. For instance, a younger couple may be looking toward finding new career opportunities or saving for a new home or that new baby. Families with children will have goals related to providing for the kids and getting them through school. Couples whose children have left home face different financial challenges. So you can't compare your goals to others' unless they are in the same life situation.

Prioritize each item in all three lists. Which ones are the most important goals to pursue?

Determine Income

The next step is to determine the amount of income your family has. You need to know how much money you have to spend. But be sure you are matching the amount you have to spend during a certain period of time to the same period of time for which you have written goals.

Most budgets are written for a 12-month period, usually starting in January. There are several good reasons to do it on a calendar year basis. Most budgets and billing periods, like credit cards and loans, are on 12-month cycles which begin in January. The tax year for most people begins in January. But if you want to start your 12 months at a different time, that's fine.

If you're just starting out, I suggest writing a budget for the first six months with a plan to review it three months from the time you start. You'll need to keep reviewing and adjusting your budget as you familiarize yourself with your spending and income patterns. It's work to do this! But don't put it off or get discouraged. It will get easier as the months go by. And you do want to rid yourself of those nagging bills, don't you?

If your income is fairly regular, it should be easier to forecast how much you will earn in the next 12 months. If it's irregular, then base your estimate on previous income and your best guess of what the future holds. If you work part-time or seasonally, or you're a salesperson on commission or self-employed, be conservative and figure the minimum amount of income you expect over the next 12 months. The principle here is to underestimate your income and plan spending against that figure. If things turn out better than you expected, great! Now that you have the income figure, let's figure expenses.

Determine Expenses

Before you start planning for future expenses you need to understand how you spent money in the past. Although your past spending was not planned, it did follow a definite pattern. You get used to spending money a certain way, on certain things. So the very first step in determining expenses is to document past spending patterns.

If you have records (your checkbook or receipts will work), you can get to it rather quickly, although these records won't tell you how you spent the cash. If you didn't keep receipts, or your checkbook doesn't tell you exactly what you spent the money for, then what you should do first, before creating a budget, is to spend the next two or three months keeping a record of spending.

Start at the beginning of the month and write down everything. This means you'll be a lot more detailed in your checkbook in stating what the check was for. If you are spending cash, you'll need to write that down, too. Why not keep a tablet near the door where you come into the house? As soon as you walk in, even before taking off your coat, write the date, the amount of cash spent, and what it was for. Don't spend a lot of time trying to organize the information, or you'll get discouraged. Just write it down.

Expenses fall into four major areas:

FIXED
Taxes
Mortgage or Rent
Loan payments
Tithing
Savings

FLEXIBLE
Food
Telephone
Utilities

OCCASIONAL
Insurance Premiums
Taxes not withheld
Tuition
Medical

DISCRETIONARY
Clothing
Gifts
Entertainment
Recreation

Put all your expenses into these four areas. (If you want to keep the division more simple, just divide expenses into two—those expenses that are fixed and those that are variable.)

There are different categories into which you can put your expenses. Listed below are the ones most often used with examples of the kinds of expenses you would put into that category. You may, however, want to include others. Go ahead. The point is to make your budget, the way you understand and can manage it.

Typical budget categories include:

Auto: gasoline, maintenance, car wash, accessories
Children: clothes, toys, supplies
Clothing
Contributions
Entertainment/Recreation: plays, ball games, concerts, eating out, vacations
Food
Gifts: birthdays, anniversaries, Christmas
Household: paint, dishes, furnishings, yard/garden
Insurance: auto, home, life, medical
Loans/Fixed Payment: mortgage/rent, auto, installment, personal
Medical: doctor, hospital, clinic, prescription/drugs
Personal: subscriptions, makeup, deodorant, personal things not fitting other categories
Savings
Taxes
Tithe: different from contributions in that it comes off the top of income. More on this later.
Utilities: electricity, gas, water, garbage, telephone
Miscellaneous: anything not fitting other categories

Decide if you are happy with the way you are currently spending your money. Did you spend too much in any area? Spending reveals priorities and values you hold. Are your priorities and values right? Do you feel right about your spending patterns?

Next, consider what you are going to do in tithing and saving money. The Scriptures state that the tithe is the Lord's. Some people interpret the tithe as 10 percent of your income before taxes. Others as 10 percent after taxes. Some view it as proportionate giving.

Richard Foster states that the tithe is "an Old Testament principle that should be a standard we will not go below except in the rarest of circumstances. This is not a rigid law, but a starting point for organizing our economic lives." [1]

The principle is to give back to the Lord what He has given you before you start deciding how else to spend your money. After you've settled tithing, move directly to saving. Saving should also come off your income before you make other spending decisions. If you can get yourself to do these two things, you'll be way down the path toward being in control of your money.

Now you're ready to create a budget. Here are the steps:

1. Put down the amount you've allocated for tithing and savings.

2. Put down the amount for each fixed expense. This includes loans, rent or mortgage, any bill for the same amount that comes due every month.

3. Take every periodic expense, like insurance, medical, tuition, car maintenance payments. Make sure you know the annual cost of each. Divide it by 12 months and put that monthly amount into savings. If you have only a few months until a payment is due, then divide the amount by the number of months until it's due.

Example:

Cost per year	*To savings each month*
Insurance $360	$30
Average cost of car repair $180	$15
School supplies for Bobby $120	$10
Usual taxes due in April $480	$40
Unplanned last year $600	$50
Christmas last year $900	$75
Health checkups last year $240	$20

Now you have two sections in savings: That amount you've put away that is general in nature (under 1 above) and the other that contains funds for all the periodic expenses. This should prevent some unpleasant surprises at bill-paying time.

4. Put down every other expense not covered by the points above. Don't forget to add fun money for every member of the family—money each can use any way he or she wants—money that doesn't need to be accounted for.

Now you have what you think you should spend in each category. Add all the figures and compare the number to your income figure. If you're like most people, your expense figure will be far more than your income. Don't be alarmed. This is where you begin the exciting journey toward getting control of your money!

Get the family back together for a problem-solving session. Begin in prayer, asking God to help each of you discover where to trim. Then jump in. What expenses can you reduce? What can you postpone or drop altogether? What spending patterns can you change? Maybe you can drive less and not have to buy as much gas for the car. Or maybe you can get more creative in your grocery shopping, buying more basic foods rather than expensive luxury items. Perhaps you can get those shoes resoled rather than buy a new pair, or make use of free educational/recreation services rather than maintain a membership in the local club.

Look at the expenses critically and objectively. If you don't have enough money for your daily needs, you'll have to find a way to reduce fixed expenses, such as moving to a less expensive home or apartment, or shopping for just as good but less expensive insurance, or getting rid of the gas guzzler and driving an economy car. After you've done all of this, consider new sources of revenue, such as a spouse working or the children involved in baby-sitting or newspaper routes, etc. Do this last, since you want to be sure you've cut expenses and not just gone out and increased income to maintain poor spending patterns.

This is the point where you need again to introduce spiritual values and goals. What are you doing with your life? What does God want for you? What should be important? Remember, if you choose to ignore these issues so you can keep spending, they may go away for a time, but will quickly come back.

Deal realistically with the choices you're making. You can't economize on values. Follow the right ones and you'll be happy.

Working the Plan

Keep good records of where the money went. Put all receipts in a box. Write down every cash expense the moment you step in the door of your home or apartment. Put those credit card slips in one place. (Remember a credit card slip is money spent. A safe way to deal with it is to put the actual amount you charged in savings so when the bill comes in you've got the money to pay. Better yet, don't use the credit card.) To make it really fun, get the family together once a week to talk about how you're doing. Add up all the expenses by category, and report on the progress.

At month's end, reevaluate your budget, making small adjustments to make it compatible with reality. If you discover some extra money, put it away. Your budget will reflect you. You should revise it at least every six months since circumstances will change. Just keep in mind that you won't have a perfect budget the first time around. Keep at it. Know that freedom from uncontrolled spending is just around the corner!

Lastly, be aware of what Richard Foster calls the spiritual reality of money. "Behind money are invisible spiritual powers, powers that are seductive and deceptive, powers that demand an all-embracing devotion. It is this fact that the apostle Paul saw when he observed that 'the love of money is the root of all evils' (I Tim. 6:10)."[2] True freedom comes from the daily disciplines of budgeting and control coupled with a keen awareness of the spiritual forces at work.

CHAPTER FIVE

COUNSELING THE PERSON IN CRISIS

F OR A PERSON IN TROUBLE, THE JOURNEY BACK TO FINANCIAL wholeness usually cannot be done alone. The person needs someone to talk to, someone to help. This is where you come in.

Begin by understanding how and why the person got into trouble in the first place. People who have financial problems usually fall into four major categories:
1. They are victims of an uncontrollable situation.
2. They have a poor self-image.
3. They are pursuing humanistic/materialistic values.
4. They have beliefs that cause the problem.

These are the four areas we will explore in this chapter. First, we will consider how to determine what the root cause is and what major area it falls into. Then we'll look at how to deal with the problems one on one.

The problems we humans have can rarely be easily defined. Causes overlap and solutions need to be broad and far-reaching. For instance, the problem of the person you're dealing with may have come to the surface through the loss of a job (an uncontrollable situation). But as you investigate, you find a poor self-image, and a list of beliefs which together with everything else has predetermined financial failure. In this case you would have to draw advice from three different sections of this chapter and apply it in one situation.

We need to acknowledge the complexity of people's problems. This book provides some patterns or suggestions to follow. Don't use them dogmatically. Each case will be different, and you will need to rely on the Holy Spirit's help in every case.

Before we get into specific guidance for counseling situations I want to step back and give you a broad perspective on money, what it is, and what it means to people.

What Is Money?

Our world is made up of resources. For our purposes here, we'll divide these resources into two distinct groups: human and natural. The human resource is labor, which if directed toward other people results in service. Labor combined with natural resources results in goods and products, which make up what our world looks like and what it uses to survive and give itself pleasure.

Hundreds of years ago people exchanged labor and other resources to acquire things they needed. This process could have been witnessed in any marketplace. There, with the barter system, a woven basket could be traded for two pounds of potatoes and some meat. As the population grew, there was an increase and diversity of products and services. Barter became impractical and that's how money emerged as a way to acquire products and services.

In an effort to survive and enhance their lives, people through the years have been constantly producing more services, products, and goods. These are sold to other people. Even natural resources are sold. That's why you can buy a piece of vacation property next to a lake or the land your house is on.

If you step back and analyze it, in all of these transactions, labor is the first and primary thing we really own. And labor is a gift from God. Labor generates money. Money is used to purchase goods, products, and services which in turn can be combined with other resources to create new goods, products, and services and be given to someone else for money.

So money represents the value of a resource. It's used as a way of transferring value from one place to another. There is no other purpose for money. Money is still the fruit of our labor. It represents hard work and emotional investment. The work for which it was exchanged bears the imprint of our personalities. Like it or not, there is a lot of us tied up in our money!

What Money Means to People

Every statement about and action pertaining to money speaks to how we value ourselves and each other. Why do people compare how much they make? Why do we work so hard to get money? Why does it feel so good to have money? In our society money is one way we can show we have value as people. And since money buys things, the more things we have also says something about our worth.

Why does it feel so good to go shopping? Why does the mere act of buying something make our problems go away momentarily? Because just the ability to make something that is not ours suddenly become ours "proves" our own value and power. It also distracts us from the problems or anxieties we are facing. Why do people have a difficult time talking about money? Because so much of us is tied up in it. We always want to know how much a person paid for something, yet we resent being asked the same question.

How we spend our money says almost everything about who we are and what we value.

Our use of money:

Shows what our commitments are. If we spend a lot of it on eating out and entertainment, on clothes, gadgets, etc., then we may love giving ourselves pleasure. If we spend it on others, like relatives and friends, we may be showing our love or buying theirs. If we give it to strangers in need, we may be showing compassion and mercy. How we spend our money often shows what we are committed to and what we value.

Makes statements of power and control. If we always need to pick up the tab, if we need to make more than our spouse, if we need to make or initiate all purchase decisions, if we only give money to those causes that allow us to be part of the decision making, if all or some of these statements are true, then we use money as a symbol of power and control in life.

Shows the level of our self-esteem. If we are constantly buying clothes, accessories, makeup, and spending money on the care of hair and skin beyond reasonable need, we may be trying to dress up a sagging self-image. And if we are frequently replacing items that do not need replacement such as home appliances, office accessories, furniture, even things like rugs, paint, dishes, and lawns, we may be buying status or trying to avoid anxious feelings.

The use of money is the clearest way you can tell the most about a person. People use money in so many ways to achieve rational, intelligent goals as well as emotional ones. For instance, look at this partial list of goals people might have in their use of money:

To help them forget about their problems. They go shopping and spend money, it feels so good when the mind is focused on something pleasant. It's like having been asleep. Those nagging feelings, those nasty voices, that knot in the pit of the stomach just wasn't there, and, oh, how good it feels!

To get even. A spouse has offended him or her, or has restricted the person. He or she got cheated in that last pay review. Or if a person is in a divorce proceeding, he or she may spend as much as possible to leave the bills with the person who deserves them.

To avoid disappointing someone else. The sister couldn't afford giving a present to her mom, so she went out and charged the purchase on her credit card. The parent just couldn't bear to be outdone and buys the kids things they don't need.

To be like the Joneses. They can't let the neighbors have a better car, the peers at work have better clothes, the friends at church take a better vacation.

To express anger. They'll leave that "wayward" child out of the will, only give a gift to one of the brothers, not invite the aunt and uncle to the expense-paid weekend. They'll give to the anti-smoking or anti-war charity.

To express love. They'll give to people in need. They'll pay for a trip across town or across the country for a special person or give generous gifts and money to a lot of people.

To pursue a hobby. The person may be a camera buff, into computers, handcrafts, sewing, painting. But the hobby is so prominent in the person's life that it is difficult not to spend when an item in that special interest group becomes available.

To postpone or avoid payment. The person may believe that by using a credit card he or she really doesn't have to pay. That paying is a future event with a strong possibility of never arriving.

To gain acceptance. The person couldn't really afford to pay for the meal, but something inside made him do it. The party was coming up and a new dress was needed.

To take care of needs. The person uses money to provide for his or her basic needs and those of the family.

To do good. The person sees unmet needs in the world and uses money to help. This act is motivated by love, religious beliefs, and sometimes as a "vote" against a government or system, a policy, or just evil.

To maintain a habit. It could be eating, buying drugs, any behavior that we've become addicted to.

Money means a lot to people. And it's a very powerful force in our world. It buys people, things, and even feelings. It can be used as an instrument of destruction and evil and can do the greatest good. We love money, much more than we should, that's why we get into trouble with it so easily.

Your challenge, as a Christian leader and counselor, is to help Christians understand money, love it less, use it more wisely, and get out of the problems they currently have with it. It's not an easy job. But remember, when dealing with money you're not just dealing with dollar bills, coins, and debt. You're dealing with the very hearts and souls of people, because money means much more to them than many can possibly admit.

Counseling People—Some Practical Suggestions

Objective of the first session: To uncover the real problem and comfort the person.

Great care must be taken during this first session to make the person feel comfortable with telling you what has happened. Avoid offering advice. At the beginning of the session, state that all you want to do this first time is understand what has happened.

Even if you think the solution is easy, take the time to have two sessions rather than one. The first should be used to understand and comfort the person, the second to get into practical help. A lot of progress can be made if the person has a chance to think about what he or she has told you. This think time, between the first and second session, is critical toward helping the person be part of the solution.

Also, during this session, show love to the person. He or she may have just gone through a frightening and difficult experience. The person may be wondering what God is up to. Each may have feelings about Him that are difficult to allow and even more difficult to verbalize. He or she is hurting. Talk about the feelings; let the anger come out. But don't give advice. Just listen. In fact, before starting this session, ask God to help you be a good listener and comforter. You'll have the urge to jump in with solutions, but don't! Hold that tongue and just simply listen and love.

Format of the first session: First of all, before the person even arrives, spend some time in prayer, asking God to help you be a good listener and comforter, and to give you insight into what will be said. If you know the person and have feelings or judgments residing in your heart about him or her, this is also good material to take to God. As much as possible you want to have a clean slate for that child of God who will walk into your office.

Be sure your phone has been routed or taken care of in some way. Be sure your spouse or anyone else who may interrupt you knows not to. You can't have a parade going through the room and expect to minister effectively to the needs of the person.

Plan to have everything under control so you can direct all of your attention to the person coming to you for help. Make sure you have pencil and paper in hand to take notes. Don't rely on your memory. Plan to write down as much as you can. Don't use a tape recorder. It is threatening to have everything you've said on permanent record.

When the person arrives, greet him or her warmly and kindly. If you haven't taken your coat off, do so. You need to be relaxed and open. Don't sit behind a desk. Instead, have a couple chairs out in front of it and place them at angles. They shouldn't be directly facing each other.

Begin your session with prayer. Then state that all you want to do today is understand the person's situation. Ask, "How can I help?" rather than saying something like, "Now, what's the problem?" You are there to help more than hear a problem. During the course of finding out how to help you'll discover the problem.

Keep asking questions until you are sure you understand what the problem is. Remember, it's not necessary to give advice this first session. When you are done asking questions and you believe you understand what the problem is ask the person what he or she thinks the problem is. But do this by asking for an explanation as to how the person got into this situation. Then close in prayer and schedule the next meeting.

The objective of your counseling following the first session: To get the person to understand and accept the real reason for the problem and to do something about it.

Note the emphasis on the three key words in the statement above. To understand, accept, and do something about the problem. Each action springs from the one before it. In a specific situation you may want to consider these three points the major categories of your counseling. Take the person through understanding, then accepting, then agreeing to the steps he or she needs to take to solve the problem.

For Uncontrollable Situations:

When a force outside a person's life causes something bad to happen, it's difficult to believe that people are good or even that God is good. Anger is usually the result. Let's start with an example:

Janice has just been promoted to the job of her dreams. She is on her way to work when a drunk driver swerves into her lane and crashes into her. The resulting injuries force Janice to remain in the hospital for three weeks, and after that, bedridden at home for two months. Her employer, unsure of her recovery and not willing to wait the needed time, fills her slot with another person. Janice's old position is covered so well during her absence that the company decides to eliminate it. Janice has lost her job.

The Understanding Sessions: Janice is angry and hurt. Allow her to express it. She is mad at the drunk driver. She's mad at the courts for not being harsher on drunk drivers. She's mad at the person who "took" her job, the person that covered her old one, and the employer who decided she wasn't needed. She's mad at God. She's wondering why He could allow such a thing to happen.

She's worried about her future, about the insurance settlement, about money. She's lonely. She thought a lot more people would care more about her through her ordeal than really did. And she has a list of the people that she is disappointed in— people who had always said they would be there when she needed them, but who weren't!

Your only task the first session (or more if it takes longer) is to let Janice express it all. Help her do it. If she says something that isn't quite right or appropriate, don't correct her or say, "You really shouldn't feel that way." Just let her talk. Every once in a while, as she is talking, state that you understand what she is saying, or that you understand how she could feel that way.

The Accepting Sessions: By now you've had Janice express all of her feelings. And you've allowed her to say anything she wants. Something terrible has happened to her and she is angry and hurt. Now it's time to help her accept the situation.

You are now trying to help Janice make the transition from the paralysis of anger and hurt to doing something constructive. This will take a long time, so be patient. Ask her to give an explanation for what has happened. You should be prepared to give your explanation. If you were giving an explanation you might say something like this:

"I know this has been difficult for you, Janice. And a lot of people have hurt you. You thought you could depend on them, and you couldn't. But a lot of people did pull through for you. Let's list them. (Go through list of people.) A lot worse could have happened. But it didn't. You could have been paralyzed for life. Or killed. You are alive and well. God didn't single you out. A man, exercising his free will that God has also given you and me, got drunk and lost control. You were there. And this employer didn't act honorably. Yes, a lot of terrible things have happened—all started by an accident, something out of your control. Now we should sit down and figure out what to do about it."

Yes, this explanation is simplistic, but it does communicate the tone and principles involved. At some point you need to make the transition from the free release of emotion and hurt to a constructive look at the future. In this case, Janice needs to think soon about a job.

The Doing Sessions: By now, in Janice's life, a lot of time has gone by, and income is certainly becoming a factor in the quality of her life. You need to determine the practical steps she will take and when she must take them.

This last series of sessions should be geared to agreeing on a course of action. For a person out of work because of an accident, loss of health, or reduction in work force, the first step is updating the resumé, or if one doesn't exist, creating one. If you don't feel comfortable assisting in this process, ask a business person in your church, familiar with resumés and employment procedures, if he or she would be willing to help.

If you can't find help in your church write to INTERCRISTO, a Christian career guidance organization, at 19303 Fremont Avenue North, Seattle, WA 98133.

A lack of a steady source of income can be a major additional cause of stress for the victim of an uncontrollable situation. And that situation may be anything from the collapse of the bank where the person had money, to the house burning down. There must be a reliable source of income. As soon as possible, after passing the emotional stage in your counseling, move to solve this problem.

For Poor Self-Image:

A poor self-image can be a very difficult counseling situation. Difficult because the person cannot admit to feeling bad about who he or she is. And since acceptance precedes doing something about the problem you must seek it first. Let's go to another example to help put realism into this situation.

John has just lost his job. It's the third job he's had in a year. And he's come to you for help. When he comes to your office you notice he is immaculately dressed, is driving a late-model sports car, has expensive jewelry on, and there's not one hair out of place. He's a man who seems to be confident and in control. When you ask him what has happened, he explains that he could not put up with the dishonesty in his boss, that his constant habit of unethical business practices has finally been too much to handle. So John just quit!

The Understanding Sessions: As you dig deeper into why John has quit his job, you discover that what John has labeled unethical was simply his boss' decision to exclude him from an upcoming series of planning meetings. When they had first talked about it, John's boss had said he was considering including him. Now, as things had progressed, John's boss had decided not to include him. The reason: John, in his opinion, was too focused on getting involved in everyone else's business and needed to spend more time on the work he was hired to do. John charged that his boss had lied. The escalation resulted in John quitting.

But rather than leave it there, you probe further:

Counselor: "Was this the only reason you quit?"

John: "No, people in that office really don't care about me. I was trying to be helpful in many areas of the company that I believe needed my help. But everywhere I went to help, people didn't cooperate. I think my boss had something to do with it."

Probing further you ask what happened in the job before this one and you discover a similar pattern. In every job, John had tried to dominate and push himself on others. In every job a blowup had occurred and John had either quit or been asked to leave.

You can see by the story so far that you must continue to ask questions until you come to an understanding of what has been happening in the person's life. In this case, John has not been able to do the job he was hired to do. As soon as he gets inside an organization, he takes steps to involve himself where he shouldn't, all to prove that he is a valuable person.

Counselor: "John, what's the most important thing in life to you?"

John: "I'd have to say it's people. People that care. I'm no dummy, you know. But sometimes people treat me like I am. And that gets me really mad! I feel really good when I can help someone else out."

Counselor: "You used the word *dummy*. Did someone actually call you that?"

John (hangs his head): "My dad used to call me a dummy all the time. He said I'd never be like my older brother Bill. And that he'd be surprised if I ever amounted to much. Bill and Dad were really good friends, and I guess I just felt left out."

As the conversation develops, you discover that Bill has spent his lifetime trying to measure up. You talk further, and find Bill is critically in debt. He has bought most everything he owns on credit and has no way to pay it back. And many of his purchases are his attempt to make himself a better person.

You have reached the final point of understanding. What started as an issue of unemployment has become, at its core, a self-image problem. The result has been chronic unemployment and compulsive spending.

The Accepting Sessions: Your task in these sessions is to help the person see and accept the connection between poor self-image and the problems he or she is currently facing.

If the problem is serious and you are not a trained counselor, you may want to suggest that the person seek professional help.

The goal is to convince the person of personal value. If the person can value self and discover that he or she no longer has to push himself or herself on others or compulsively buy things like John did to make himself feel better, then you are well on your way to really helping.

The most practical way to do this is to review what the person said during the first series of sessions and ask for opinions on the causes for the negative behavior. In John's case you would state that you're sure he has been thinking about your earlier conversations and that you'd like to know what he thinks are the reasons for his quitting three different jobs during the last year.

Your goal would be to get the person to make the connection you have already seen. He or she needs and wants to be valued and that is the major reason for getting in trouble at work.

Having made that connection, you move to why he or she buys so much. Make it your goal to have the person verbalize that buying makes him or her feel more valuable.

Once you have achieved that kind of acceptance, you are ready to move on to problem solving. Be sure during this process of acceptance to be extremely gentle, patient, and kind. This is not to suggest that at other times you should be less so. It's just that gaining acceptance for the real causes is a delicate and sensitive process. Your time in prayer and preparation will be rewarded as you see the person quietly face himself or herself in a new way.

The Doing Sessions: There are three problems in John's case: poor self-image, no job, and debt. Since he has had three jobs in the last year, it should not be too hard for him to get another. The challenge is keeping it!

Since many poor self-image problems show themselves as impulsive, negative behavior, try to convince the person to curb the impulsiveness first. This way, the urge to lash out at persons who are not valuing properly will not occur. In a case like John's, you might suggest that he always place a night between his need to "force" someone to value him and the actual act. The night may put things in perspective.

He should also have a friend who will hold him accountable in behaving properly with his peers at work. John may have to report all the clashes every week and explain why they occurred. This kind of accountability, coupled with the wait period for impulsive behavior, may be the two things that stop it and help John on his way toward behaving properly at work.

While this is going on, a person like John should be reading the Scriptures that show God's love and concern for him. You might suggest a habit of consistent prayer, that God would help him love himself as God loves him.

John must uncover his value and curb his excessive behavior. Secondly, he must reduce debt and stop using credit.

For Humanistic, Self-oriented Values:

This person is different from the one with a poor self-image. He or she is motivated toward acquisition and money because of high self-orientation.

This person lives to advance his or her career as much as possible, acquire a multitude of possessions, and enjoy life to its fullest. Often God and spiritual growth take second place in this person's life—if indeed God places at all.

If a person has a self-orientation, then he or she feels that every problem can be solved through self-efforts alone. Buried deep in the heart is a margin of doubt about God's ability or participation in the lives of people.

People exhibiting this behavior are often people who have pulled themselves up from poverty or bad childhood situations. They have solved almost every problem on their own. They are independent and confident. They have an attitude that says: "I don't need anyone. I never did. I never will."

You know things are really bad if a person like this comes to you for help. The perfect job that was lost. Or the marriage fell apart. The daughter got pregnant or the son that blew his mind on drugs. Or it could be a thing of the heart. Life just doesn't have meaning. Money is no longer enough.

The Understanding Sessions: There is nothing wrong with a strong work ethic or desire to get ahead. But it dare not become life's controlling purpose, untempered by Christian values.

Whatever the situation, your objective is to understand how and why the person got into the situation. You could ask questions.
1. Why do you think you're in the situation you're in?
2. What are the deeper causes for the decisions you made?
3. What drives you to pursue advancement, possessions, and money?
4. What is really important to you in life?

Remember, you're trying to understand, and you are also trying to help the person think more analytically about the crisis situation. For the person who is wrapped up in humanistic and self-oriented values, you must keep pursuing why the person is driven toward acquisition and money. Until you get that answer you have not arrived at a point of understanding.

You'll know you've arrived at that point when the person says something as honest and direct as: "I just love to have money and things. They bring me a lot of satisfaction. And I'll do most anything to get them."

Or it may be a little more subtle: "I'm really afraid of what the future might bring, so I want to make sure I'm prepared for any situation. I know I overdo it sometimes, but I'm just not going to be left without."

The Accepting Sessions: We have already covered how to help people accept the cause of the financial problems they have. For persons holding a humanistic and self-oriented philosophy of life, pay particular attention to their need to be self-sufficient. During your conversations there will be the constant struggle between their wanting your advice and wanting to project an attitude that says, "I don't need your advice."

In these cases you must gently show the connections between the attitude and the current problem you are dealing with. Be particularly sensitive not to dominate the conversation, and if you can't make the connection right away, wait a week and try again.

The goal of the acceptance sessions is to help the person discover that the situation he or she is currently in is indeed the result of a philosophy of life, the pursuit of material values.

As a Christian, that philosophy must be converted to one in which the person's pursuit is toward maturity in Christ.

"In the power of the Holy Spirit we conquer and capture money and put it into service for Christ and his kingdom. We know that well-being is not defined by wealth, and so we can hold all things lightly—owning without treasuring, possessing without being possessed. We use money within the confines of a properly disciplined spiritual life, and we manage money for the glory of God and the good of all people."[1]

The Doing Sessions: Keep in mind that the person believes that true happiness will come from the acquisition of things and the accumulation of money.

The object is to get the person to change his or her mind. This is a spiritual goal as well as an intellectual one. Here are several suggestions:

1. Involvement in a Bible study group where Biblical values are explored. This study may be topical or may involve a verse-by-verse study of a book like Job or Proverbs.

2. A discipline of prayer where the person is asking God to reveal His mind and His values.

3. One-on-one discussions with other Christians this person would respect, either because of what the person has accomplished or been through. With the person's permission, you would contact the other party and explain the goal of the meeting: to model discovery of God's values and have those become predominant.

For Problem-causing Beliefs:

Some Christians believe that one of God's major goals is to make them prosperous.

In the Christian culture you can see this played out by people who say: "Give out of your need." "Plant a seed." The whole "seed-faith" movement *starts from truth* but can very easily be misunderstood. The truth is that we as Christians must have faith as that of a child's. Faith can do great things. We will reap what we sow. These things are *true*. What is not truth is that faith can legitimately be used as a means to become prosperous or to acquire material things, that the motive for employing faith is to have material gain (Jas. 4:3).

Our focus is to be on God, His character, His holiness, and righteousness and on how we can be instruments of His here on earth. We are to seek first the Kingdom, not the added things that may come after seeking His Kingdom (Mt. 6:33).

Because the Spirit of God is resident in a Christian's life, he is able to draw power for decision making and motivation that the non-Christian can't. He also has different values. There is no doubt that a person's relationship with Jesus Christ can make him or her a better marriage partner, a better worker, a better citizen. There is no truth to the claim, however, that because of that relationship the person will necessarily have more material possessions or suffer less hardship.

Travel to the countryside of Haiti, the barrios of Rio de Janiero, the slums of Lima, Peru, the streets of Calcutta, India, or to the rural areas of Bangladesh, Pakistan, or Nepal. Go to the island of Palau Bidong off of Malaysia for a visit with the Vietnamese refugees. I've been to all of these places, and I've seen Christians in absolute poverty.

Once you've met them you come away with the strong conviction that God is not the "cosmic bellhop in the sky," the purveyor and guarantor of material blessings to every Christian on the face of the earth.

The Understanding Sessions: The first thing is to determine what the problem is. Is the person:

1. Giving a lot of money away believing it will come back many-fold and now having financial problems?

2. Spending a lot of money, buying many things on credit, or making business decisions in an effort to "cause" prosperity?

3. Suffering emotionally because of the pressure of peers and friends who claim he or she isn't living a "victorious life" which is evidenced by the lack of prosperity?

The Accepting Sessions: The major challenge in these sessions will be to get the person to separate what is true about his or her beliefs from what is not true. The core belief itself is not what is usually wrong. It's what is attached to or woven into it. Questions like these may help the person see the situation in a new, helpful light:

What Scriptures have you studied for yourself on prosperity? Consider them again in context. Also look for New Testament models on how the disciples and early Christians lived. How does their experience parallel what you are expecting God to do in your own situation? How do you want people to relate to you? In what ways do the things you have acquired help or hinder your relationship goals?

The Doing Sessions: Set up an ongoing program that will allow the person to benefit from your and other Christians' spiritual maturity.

1. Involve the person in a Bible study, perhaps one centered on money, or on methods of inductive Bible study. Train the Christian to think for himself or herself.

2. Get the person involved in a service project with poor or oppressed Christians. Let the person see and hear firsthand about the faith and joy and pains of Christians who have never even dreamed of prosperity. If a person-to-person service is impossible, consider recommending biographies of missionaries and third-world Christians.

3. Set up regular meetings with the person. When you are attempting to restructure someone's life philosophy, the change will not come easily or quickly.

I have not addressed situations where the person who has financial problems is physically or emotionally handicapped. If a specific situation is not addressed in this book, consult a local Christian counseling or financial planning ministry or refer the person to the local office of the National Foundation for Consumer Credit (Headquarters: (301)589-5600) or the local office of Family Service America (Headquarters: (414)359-2111). Both of these organizations are dedicated to helping people get back on their feet financially. Call them with confidence.

CHAPTER SIX

PERSONAL FINANCIAL CRISIS AND YOUR WHOLE CHURCH

TOM KENNEY HAS A PROBLEM. IT BEGAN ONE FRIDAY AFTERnoon three months ago, when his foreman at the paper mill handed him a paycheck—a *final* paycheck. Tom was being laid off. The economy and paper prices were the cause, the foreman said; he had nothing but praise for Tom's work in the warehouse.

The foreman's compliments were nice, but Tom wasn't listening to them very closely. He was fighting a wave of panic, trying to think of a way to provide for his wife and two preschoolers. Numbly he shook the foreman's outstretched hand, got his lunchbox from his locker, and walked out of the plant. It was probably the last time he would do that, he knew, since rumor had it that this mill might soon shut down.

Since then, Tom and his wife Danette have found that unemployment compensation doesn't go far. Tom hates standing in line "like a bum or something" every week at the State Employment Office to collect his meager check. No job is in sight, and the family's savings have dried up. Tom's nerves are as tight as his finances; he's starting to yell at his wife and children, slamming the door as he leaves each weekday on a fruitless job search.

Danette cries often these days. She worries that the kids will get sick, since the family is no longer covered by health insurance. She worries that other customers at the supermarket will see that she is having to use food stamps. She worries about her faith, too. At first she and Tom prayed for a job, but now they wonder, "What's the point?"

So far the crisis has not kept the Kenneys from going to church. They sit in their usual pew and sing the hymns. They listen to the announcements about the Young Couples' Beach Trip ("Bring $25 per couple to cover the boat ride") and the special offering for a new grand piano. They feel left out when they hear these things; they have no money for beach trips, and

69

they wonder why the church needs a new piano when the Kenneys can't afford to get the muffler on their car fixed. When the pastor talks about "the wonderful blessings God has showered upon our nation," the Kenneys feel like unblessed, second-class Christians.

Tom and Danette have not told anyone in their congregation of 400 about their financial crisis and the pain it has brought. A few people in their Sunday School class know that Tom lost his job, and at first they let him know how badly they felt about it. "Wow, that's rough," they said. "We'll sure pray about it." But as Tom's unemployment drags on, the sympathy has turned to skepticism, even irritation. In others' eyes Tom seems to read the question, "Haven't you gotten a job *yet?*"

Danette supposes the church must have some sort of fund to help the needy, but is too embarrassed to ask anyone about it. Besides, she knows Tom would never take "charity"; he argued against the food stamps for days before finally giving in. And even if the church gave them a one-time "handout," what would the family do after that?

This Sunday morning the Kenneys did not feel up to singing the hymns ("O Happy Day" and "There's a Sweet, Sweet Spirit in This Place"). Tom barely heard as the pastor delivered a message entitled, "More Blessed to Give." Tom was preoccupied, wondering what he would do when the tires on his car finally gave out. He was also wondering whether Danette would be upset if he said he didn't want to go to church anymore—not this church, at least.

Financial Crisis: Suffering in Silence

Why are the Kenneys enduring their financial crisis without the help of their church? In a sense, they have chosen to do so. Like many—perhaps most—in our success-obsessed culture, they believe money problems are too personal to share with others. To say, "Excuse us, but we're broke," would make them feel naked, far too vulnerable to the judgments others might make.

But in another sense the Kenneys are *forced* to suffer alone and in silence. Many of their fellow church members would probably *prefer* that families like the Kenneys keep such problems to themselves. These Christians, though they likely would not admit it even to themselves, do not want to face the difficult questions raised by money problems. For example:

- Is it right for some Christians to have far more money and possessions than others do?
- What is a church's financial obligation to its members—and nonmembers?
- Should a church advise a financially strapped family to change direction, amend its life-style, move away?
- Are money problems, especially chronic ones, a sign of God's disfavor?
- How can a large group of believers truly know the needs of every member?
- If a financial problem is caused by poor money management or even sin, should the church require counseling or discipline?
- How many people can a church afford to help?
- Do members have to keep "feeling badly" for those in financial crisis when the crisis lasts for months or even years?
- Should a church sponsor activities which are too expensive for some members to take part in?

These are hard questions. No wonder most people—and churches—avoid them. But avoiding meaningful discussion of personal financial crisis practically requires people like the Kenneys to suffer in silence.

The Squeaky Wheel

Not every churchgoer in financial crisis suffers silently, of course. Take Marta Heinrichs. She has a problem, too—a lot of them. Since coming to Central Community Church four months ago, Marta has told and retold her tale of financial woe to anyone who would listen—individually and in Sunday night service "sharing" times.

Her story varies slightly from week to week, but the basics are these: Raised in Montana by "an alcoholic father who beat me every day," Marta left home at age 18 and moved to Florida to live with her cousin Florence. There Marta worked as a secretary for about a year, but was let go "because the boss' wife was jealous of me." Soon after that, cousin Florence announced that Marta would have to move out of the apartment they shared "because Florence was a tramp who always wanted to have men over, and I was cramping her style."

With about $100 in her pocket, Marta took a bus to Philadelphia. A girlhood friend had moved there and landed a job, she said, but when Marta arrived the friend was nowhere to be found. Staying in a motel, Marta noticed a church down the street and decided to attend.

"I've always been a dedicated Christian," she told the deacon who shook her hand that first Sunday morning. When she told him her story, the deacon was confused but sympathetic. He invited Marta to stay with him and his wife until more permanent arrangements could be made.

Two weeks later, Marta had worn out her welcome at the deacon's house. She had taken and then quit a minimum-wage job in a fast-food restaurant, saying, "The manager was out to get me, no doubt about that. And who can live on minimum wage?" She had refused to help around the deacon's house, claiming she had "chronic bronchitis—the doctors can't help me, and I can't breathe the dust from vacuum cleaners and so on."

Feeling guilty but at the end of his patience, the deacon asked Marta to find another place to stay. So, with $75 from the church's Caring Fund in her purse, Marta moved in with a single woman she'd met at prayer meeting. At first the woman listened with compassion as Marta railed against the "cold-hearted" deacon for "throwing me out." But before long the cycle repeated itself, and Marta was awkwardly evicted.

At last count Marta had stayed with seven Central Community Church families in four months. The Caring Fund Committee will not give her more money; most of the deacons hope she will just go away—no doubt to another church, where the same scenario will again be played out. The pastor is sure there must be a way to help Marta, but he doesn't know what to do. Meanwhile, Marta says she isn't sure she wants to be a Christian after all—if Christians are "like the hypocrites in this church."

Educating the Church

The stories of the Kenneys and Marta are based on real events that occur often in the church. They illustrate the fact that in Christ's body, *personal financial crisis isn't just personal*. The whole church is affected—or should be. Whether that effect is positive or negative depends to a large degree on how well a congregation and its leaders have been trained to deal with money problems.

What kinds of training could have helped in these two cases?

1. Biblical teaching about money and caring could have created a more open, supportive atmosphere in the church. In such an atmosphere the Kenneys could feel free to reveal their needs, and Tom might hear about additional job prospects.

2. Classes in money management might have helped the Kenneys and Marta stretch their available dollars and avoid such severe financial crises in the future.

3. Sessions on how to help those in financial crisis could have guided church leaders to support the Kenneys instead of alienating them—and confront Marta concerning her destructive behavior.

In other words, there was a need for greater *awareness* at these churches—awareness of Biblical truth, of the needs of those in financial crisis, of money management principles, of the role of lay leaders in counseling and discipline, and of established channels for helping. You can increase such awareness in your church by finding ways to educate members and leaders.

A Long-Term Task

Educating your church in these areas may take a long time, especially since our society's selfish views of money, financial crisis, and financial aid tend to clash so starkly with the teachings of Christ. Patience and repetition will be required as you help to "raise consciousness."

You will also need to think through some tough questions—questions like those raised earlier in this chapter. Your church may not be able to reach a consensus on issues such as an appropriate standard of living, sharing of resources, responsibility to those outside the church, and the role of discipline in financial aid. But wrestling with these questions could bring spiritual growth to your fellowship if done patiently, prayerfully, and mutually.

While it would be impossible to provide complete training outlines in the space available here, the following session plans should give you a place to begin. The principles contained in them may be adapted for use in a variety of settings, including sermons, seminars, workshops, retreats, classes, and support groups. Additional resources on these subjects are listed at the end of the chapter.

Training in Biblical Principles

The Bible has a great deal to say about money and its role in our lives. Scripture also says much about the need to care for one another—a concept which should be made especially concrete at times of financial crisis. In addition to adapting material found elsewhere in this book, you may find the following session ideas helpful.

SESSION 1: MONEY ISN'T EVERYTHING

Aim: To remind members that the purpose of life is to glorify God, not to acquire money and possessions.

Filthy Lucre? Ask for definitions of money. Suggest that it's a way to transfer value, a liquid form of labor. Is money the root of all evil, or is the problem just the love of money? (See I Tim. 6:10.) Discuss examples of how money tends to corrupt people. Are people with little money generally more spiritual than those who have a lot? (Not necessarily. But having money and the "security" it brings tends to distract us from our need to get right with God, and can insulate us from seeing the needs of the poor.)

The Non-Almighty Dollar. Read I Timothy 6:17-19, in which Paul says to tell the rich to be rich in good works, generous. What good can riches do? Brainstorm five good things participants have seen done with money. Point out that wise use of money can accomplish good things; but most people prefer to spend money on themselves, with no ultimate goal other than comfort. Does money really bring comfort? Why, when we feel badly about ourselves, can buying something make us feel better? (It appeals to the senses, lends a feeling of potency, and distracts us.) Why doesn't this feeling last? (Because our real value is God-given, a value that can't be bought or turned into liquid assets like money.) Brainstorm five things money *can't* do. Read Luke 16:13, 14. How do we try to "serve" money? What can God do that money can't?

A Happy Medium. Read Proverbs 30:7-9. Why did the writer not want to be rich? (Because he might forget God.) Why did he not want to be poor? (Because it might lead him to steal.) What was his happy medium? (To receive from God just what he needed.) What does this say about our relationship to money? (If we recognize it as coming from God and do not seek to keep more than we need, we don't have to be corrupted by it.) Read

74

Matthew 16:26, which warns against gaining the world and losing one's soul. Have participants paraphrase this verse, inserting worldly gains by which they are tempted. How much power do they want money to have over them?

First Things First. Ask what things are important, according to the Lord's Prayer—without letting participants look up the prayer. (That God's Kingdom will come, that His will be done, that we receive daily bread, that we are forgiven and forgive others, that we are delivered from evil, and that sovereignty and power and glory are ascribed to God.) What then is our purpose? (To advance God's Kingdom, do His will, and glorify Him.) What is the role of money in this? (To advance God's Kingdom.) Point out that God's glory should be our first priority, and that we should take a "daily bread" approach to money—meeting needs rather than wants. Compare this passage with Matthew 6:25-34.

SESSION 2: RESISTING PPRESSURE TO SPEND AND ACQUIRE

Aim: To help participants distinguish between real needs and mere wants created by advertising and peer pressure.

The Rising Standard. Have a few prechosen people recall how their life-styles and possessions have changed over the years as their incomes have risen. Why did things change? Did their needs change, or just their wants? What influenced their wants? Be prepared to share honestly yourself to encourage discussion.

Buy, Buy, Buy. If possible, split into three groups. Have Group 1 listen to a few TV or radio commercials you've recorded, or examine ad sections from a recent Sunday newspaper. Ask: What do these advertisers want you to do? What do they seem to promise in return for buying their products? Group 2 should discuss the problem of "keeping up with the Joneses," perhaps coming up with a humorous skit highlighting the influence of peer pressure and family expectations on buying habits. Have Group 3 discuss a case study from Chapter 2 involving a person who tried to shore up low self-esteem by spending. Then bring groups back together to share results.

Being Content. Read I Timothy 6:6-11. Discuss: With what does Paul want us to be content? Why? What are the dangers of always wanting more? Compare this passage to the three verses before it. What does this say about the seriousness of greed? Are there any today "who think godliness is a means to financial gain"?

Being Different. Read Romans 12:2, which warns against conformity to this world. How does this apply to us, to our culture? When advertisers, peers, and our own feelings of inadequacy tell us to conform, what should we do? How can our minds be renewed in this area? List the group's practical suggestions for disregarding the pressures that call us to endlessly spend and acquire.

SESSION 3: WHEN MONEY PPOBLEMS STRIKE

Aim: To explore Biblical reasons for and responses to financial crisis.

Who's to Blame? List reasons one might give for money problems (laziness, economic conditions leading to unemployment, oppression by the powerful, God's judgment, lack of planning, lack of education, mental or emotional illness, lack of self-control, etc.). Observe that any of these might apply, but God's role is of special interest to the Christian. Read Job 1:1-5. What kind of man was Job? (Blameless, upright, and rich.) Read 1:6-19. Did financial crisis befall Job because he was being punished by God? (No, it was more of a test.) Read 1:20-22. What was Job's response? (To continue to put his faith in God.) Point out that trouble is not necessarily punishment. To discover other reasons for financial crisis, see Proverbs 6:6-11; 22:28; 23:20, 21; 24:30-34; Jeremiah 22:13, 17. God is sovereign (I Sam. 2:7), but cash flow is not a gauge of spiritual condition (Eccl. 7:14).

When It Happens to You. Ask how it feels to have money trouble (scary, humiliating; produces guilt, anger, sorrow, etc.). What are possible responses? (Blame God, panic, refuse to accept "charity," ask for help, try to maintain a "successful" front, try to compensate by spending more, etc.) How do these responses compare with Job's? Split into groups, each of which faces one of the following scenarios: (a) long-term unemployment, (b) massive debt caused by excessive use of credit, or (c) overwhelming medical bills not covered by insurance. What steps could be taken to overcome these crises? Regather and discuss ideas.

When It Happens to Others. Ask each group to explain how it would feel to face the crisis it discussed. What would the victims want others to understand? To do? How difficult would it be to praise God in the situation? How would the victims react to accusations of laziness, God's judgment, lack of planning, etc.? What actions and atmosphere could help the victims to praise and trust God in the midst of crisis? Explain that the next session will focus on those actions and that atmosphere as it relates to your church. Close with prayer for those in your fellowship who face money problems.

SESSION 4: A CHURCH THAT CARES

Aim: To encourage members to care about those who have money problems, and to express that caring in helpful ways.

The Samaritan Church. Read Luke 10:25-37, about the Good Samaritan. Then have participants come up with and act out another parable—this one about a whole church that encounters a robbery victim in the front pew. Divide into three "production companies"; the first group tells the story of a bureaucratic church, the second deals with a church that condemns or ignores the needy, and the third shows what happens when a church is truly a "neighbor" to the victim. Discuss the parables. What causes the differences among churches like these?

The First Caring Church. Read Acts 2:42-47; 4:32-35. How did the early Christians treat possessions and each other? What motivated them? What was the effect on the watching world? Why are most churches today so unlike the one described in these passages? What could happen if today's Church met physical needs as the early church did?

Knocking Down the Barriers. Read I Corinthians 12:12-27. How should members of a church view each other? What happens when one part of the body hurts or is in need? Point out that meeting the needs of those in financial crisis requires both givers and receivers. What makes it hard to be a giver? (Selfishness, fear of not having enough for oneself, not knowing the needs, etc.) What makes it hard to be a receiver? (Pride, bitterness toward God or other Christians, etc.) Point out that "charity" means "love"; when love takes the form of financial aid, we should not allow pride to prevent another from expressing love to us. How can the "body" concept help us overcome these barriers?

We Have a Dream. Have church leaders, preferably after having gone through the three leaders' sessions found later in this chapter, share their visions of how your church can be more sensitive and helpful to those with money problems. Encourage others to add ideas. If possible, pass out sign-up sheets on which members can indicate their willingness to help in specific physical or financial ministries in your church.

Training in Money Management

These sessions will probably be most helpful in a workshop format, so that participants may ask questions and try out what' they've learned (making a budget, for example). As noted in the session outlines, professional financial advisors should be invited to assist if at all possible.

SESSION 1: EARNING

Aim: To promote the idea that work has value beyond the earning of money, and that earning money has meaning beyond the acquiring of things.

Why Work? Have participants imagine a world without work, in which economic needs are automatically met. What would be the effect on our bodies? Our minds? Our self-esteem? Our characters? Our relationships? Would such a world be boring or exciting? What would we miss most without work? Read the following verses and discuss the reasons given for working: Genesis 1:28 (to subdue the earth); Ecclesiastes 2:24, 25 (for satisfaction); Ephesians 4:28 (to share); II Thessalonians 3:7-12 (for food, to avoid idleness, to follow Paul's command and example, to avoid being a burden to others); I Timothy 5:8 (to provide for family); Colossians 3:23-25 (to serve God). Ask: Why doesn't the Bible mention becoming rich, famous, or powerful as reasons for work?

The Paycheck. How do working participants feel when they receive their paychecks? Why? Who do they believe owns the money they make? Point out that God is the Source of wealth, but that He entrusts it to us as He sees fit. He allows us to be stewards of it. He also allows us to "own" it; otherwise we could not truly *give* it.

The Human Resource. Invite a career counselor or personnel director to talk about ways to manage one's earning potential (through training, career planning, job choices, negotiating pay, etc.). If there are a number of unemployed people in your church, you may want to start a support group that offers training in job hunting (interviewing, resumé writing, etc.).

Fruits of Our Labors. Read Ecclesiastes 5:18, 19, observing that it is good to find satisfaction in our work and in the fruits of our work. But God is also concerned with the way we manage all the resources He entrusts to us (read the Parable of the Talents, Luke 19:11-26). Ask each person to consider: If the Lord returned as the master did and observed what you've done with your financial resources, what might He say?

SESSION 2: BUDGETING

Aim: To show participants why and how to create budgets that meet their needs and incomes.

Where Did It Go? Distribute paper and pencils. Ask participants to account for every dollar they spent last week. Then ask them to write the percentages of their incomes spent on housing, food, clothes, and savings. Chances are that group members will find it hard to pinpoint where their money has gone. Discuss how difficult it is to keep track of spending when you don't have a budget.

The Noble Budgeter. Read Proverbs 31:10-31. What actions of the "wife of noble character" relate to wise use of money? She spends wisely (vs. 16); she earns money (vss. 18, 24); she gives to those in need (vs. 20); she lives frugally by making some things rather than buying them (vs. 22). Point out that this wife carefully considers income and expenditures, the principle behind budgeting. Budgeting takes different forms for different households; the less "disposable" income you have, the more detailed should be your budget. If group members have tried budgeting, ask them to share their stories. Emphasize that people should try more than one budgeting method to see which one works best for them.

Making a Budget. Using an overhead projector or chalkboard, fill out a sample household budget to show how the process works (see Chapter 4 for instructions). Ask an accountant, banker, or other financial adviser to explain the budgeting process and "safe" percentages to budget for housing, medical care, and other expenses. If possible, ask participants a week *before* the meeting to bring records of their basic expenses so that they can spend this time filling out their own budgets and asking questions. Explain that group members may want to adjust their budgets (especially for giving and saving) after the next few sessions.

Sticking with It. Ask group members to choose a budgeting

system (ledger, running tally, separate envelopes containing allowances, etc.) to try for a month. Each member or couple should find another with whom to meet in a month to discuss results. Keep your financial advisor "on call" to help for at least a month—if not longer.

SESSION 3: GIVING

Aim: To help group members understand the importance of tithes and offerings in the practice of stewardship.

Prioritizing. Give each person a slip of paper and a pencil. Have each person write the words, "Giving," "Saving," and "Spending"—in the order in which he or she thinks money should be budgeted for those purposes. Discuss—but don't debate—the results. Encourage participants to keep an open mind on this subject during the next few sessions.

What the Giving's For. Read Proverbs 11:24, 25 and Acts 20:35. What results of giving are mentioned? (They all boil down to being blessed in some way.) Does this mean giving is "profitable," that it literally makes money? (Not necessarily. God promises only to meet our *needs,* and if He blesses us financially we are to share that with others. Compare I John 3:17, 18.) What are some nonmonetary blessings that come from giving? What blessings might result from giving to a hungry person? To one who needs work clothes? To a Sunday School that needs curriculum? To a missionary? To a youth group's refreshment fund?

Ten Percent and Counting. Split into two groups. Group 1 should examine Old Testament references to tithing (Lev. 27:30-32; Deut. 12:17; 14:22) and report findings. Group 2 should study New Testament references to the same subject (Mt. 23:23; Luke 18:9-14, 18-27) and report. What was tithed in the Old Testament? (A variety of resources, not just money.) Did people ever give beyond a tithe? (Yes.) Did Jesus do away with tithing? (Not necessarily. But He stressed the spirit over the letter of the Law, encouraging generous giving which may far exceed ten percent in many cases.) What are the implications of these passages for our giving?

Give 'til It Hurts? Read Mark 12:41-44, the story of the Widow's Mite. Discuss the term, "sacrificial giving." Does it mean "painful giving"? Compare II Corinthians 9:6-11. What kind of giver does the Lord love? (A cheerful one.) How can we give sacrificially and cheerfully? (God gives the grace and the means.) Why does He enrich us? (So that we can be generous.)

Managing Your Giving. Have your church treasurer explain ways to give, perhaps handing out copies of the church budget to show where the money goes. Discuss principles for careful giving, including these:

1. Give to your church before giving to other organizations.

2. Think through your giving rather than reacting to emotional appeals.

3. Require financial statements from the groups to which you give.

4. Don't be taken in by fund raisers who promise that you'll get more money from God if you give to them.

Optional: Examine recent fund-raising letters you've received. What appeals do they use? What questions do they leave unanswered? Study a parachurch organization's financial statement to see how much money is spent on living expenses; compare several such statements if possible.

SESSION 4: SAVING

Aim: To show why and how to set aside money for future use.

Emergency! Invite people from your church who have gone through unexpected financial crisis (the Great Depression, unemployment, losing a family farm, death of a breadwinner, major medical expenses, house fire, etc.). Have them tell how having savings in the bank helped (or could have helped) them survive their emergencies. Stress the fact that no one should assume that his or her income is assured, much less that it will grow. Saving is preparing for unforeseen expenses, for large, planned purchases, or for predictable times of lower income (such as retirement).

The Wisdom of Saving. Read Proverbs 6:6-11; 21:20; Ecclesiastes 7:12. How do these verses encourage saving? (We are to be diligent and store provision as the ant does; we should realize that poverty can strike suddenly and should prepare for it; we should store what we need for the future instead of consuming it all as soon as we get it; money is described as a shelter, and shelters protect—though wisdom preserves more effectively than does money alone.)

81

The Difficulty of Saving. Most of us save only a small percentage of what we earn. Why? (We think we need all our income now; we don't want to wait to make a large purchase; we aren't in the habit of saving.) Ask participants to tell of times when they "saved up" for something. In what ways was saving a positive experience? What fruits of the Spirit (Gal. 5:22, 23) could be developed through saving? (Perhaps the joy and peace of being content with less; patience; faithfulness; self-control.)

The Method of Saving. Point out that savings should be set aside *before* spending if at all possible. Have a financial adviser describe several ways to save (savings account, certificate of deposit, savings bond, etc.) and the advantages of each. Don't encourage members to hoard money which could be better used to help others, however; and don't assume that every member has enough disposable income to save a substantial amount. Emphasize the importance of setting aside a little at a time.

SESSION 5: SPENDING

Aim: To help participants get the most for their money and avoid excessive debt.

Mystery Auction. Hand three participants "play money" from a board game or novelty shop. They are to use the money to bid on several "mystery" items—sight unseen, because you've hidden the items in boxes. Start the bids at $10, with no upper limit. The object of the game is to end up with the items of greatest value (determined by their actual retail price). After the bidding, reveal the objects and add up the value of each person's purchases (along with money unspent) to see who wins. Discuss spending-related issues raised by the game—including the difficulty of getting the best value, and the pressures (such as hype and competition) that encourage overspending.

The Good, the Bad, and the Expensive. Read Proverbs 22:26, 27; 23:20, 21. What warnings are given concerning spending? (Avoid debt; self-indulgence and addiction lead to overspending and poverty.) Read Mark 14:3-9, the account of the woman who was criticized for pouring expensive perfume over Jesus' feet. Why was this extravagant expenditure appropriate? (It honored Jesus directly and served as a lesson to others.) Does this justify *self*-indulgent extravagance? (No.) How did Jesus answer those who said the money should have gone to the poor? (There would be many opportunities for them to help the poor, and only a few to honor Jesus in person.) Does this justify spending unnecessarily on oneself when others are in need? (No.) Discuss ways to decide whether a purchase is too extravagant (see Chapter 3 for advice on limiting spending).

Where Credit Is Due. Point out that Scripture discourages borrowing money. Have any group members been able to avoid debt entirely? (Probably not.) Invite a financial counselor to explain proper use of credit and how to get out of debt (or see Chapters 2, 3, and 7).

Household Hints. Split into small groups to come up with ways to get the most for your money in your area (best discount stores, warehouse-type supermarkets, least expensive services such as auto repair, child care, etc.). Compile the best of these suggestions and distribute copies to the whole group.

Training Church Leaders to Help

The following sessions could be used during meetings of deacons, elders, or other leaders, or as part of a leaders' retreat.

SESSION 1: OUR CHURCH WANTS TO HELP

Aim: To familiarize helpers with your church's policies and procedures for dealing with those in financial crisis.

God's Concern. Split into three groups for mini-studies of passages which make clear God's concern for those who have money problems. Group 1: James 1:27-2:13; Group 2: Deuteronomy 15:11; Proverbs 14:31; 19:17; Psalm 140:12; Isaiah 58:3-7; Ezekiel 16:49, 50; Group 3: Exodus 23:10, 11; Leviticus 19:10; 25:10-24; Deuteronomy 14:28, 29; 15:1-6; Ruth 2. Regather and discuss the overwhelming evidence of God's concern and provision for the needy. Do we share and show such concern as individuals? As a church? Why or why not?

Our Concern. With the help of appropriate church officers, explain your church's policies and procedures concerning help for those with money problems. Include policies on helping those outside your congregation, types of needs to be met by benevolent funds, making loans vs. outright gifts, access to funds, and limits on financial aid. Cover procedures including ways to discover needs, how to get approval for aid, coordination of help to avoid duplication, what to do in cases of chronic need, and how to make referrals. Distribute a list of counselors and social service agencies in your community to whom leaders may refer cases, and discuss conditions under which cases should be referred.

Showing Our Concern. Read aloud the story of the Kenneys from the beginning of this chapter. Ask: Could this have happened in our church? Why or why not? What attitudes held by the Kenneys, church members, and church leaders caused problems? How can we show greater sensitivity to those with money problems as we (1) prepare worship services and sermons, (2) plan activities, (3) raise funds for church projects, and (4) are tempted to treat people with different incomes in different ways?

SESSION 2: EVALUATING NEEDS

Aim: To help church leaders tell the truly needy from the "con artists," and to help them discern the causes of money problems.

Case Study. Read aloud the story of Marta from the beginning of this chapter. Discuss: What signals might have alerted the church not to take Marta's story at face value? (She blamed everyone but herself for her problems; she seemed overeager to tell people all the details of her story; her story varied slightly from week to week.) Which of her actions indicated poor judgment on her part, a problem which could make helping her unusually difficult? (She moved to Philadelphia with no prospect of a job; she seemed unaware of how people might react to the constant retelling of her story; she quit a job after less than two weeks.) What could the church have done to help Marta? (Assigned one person to coordinate efforts to help her and hold her accountable; checked out her story; made it clear what the church could and could not do to help her; required her to submit to church training or discipline as part of her aid "package.")

Pinpointing the Causes. Read I Thessalonians 5:14. What kinds of people are mentioned? What response is recommended for each? Point out the need to deal differently with each person; some are to be confronted, others comforted. Explain the basic reasons why people have money trouble, as outlined in Chapter 5. Using the counseling outlines in that chapter, summarize ways to deal with each type of crisis victim.

Serpents and doves. Read Matthew 10:16. How can we be both shrewd and innocent? (Shrewdness in this context implies wisdom, not deception.) Explain that we need to approach cases of financial need, especially those involving people unknown to us, with caution. Share the following suggestions for dealing with questionable cases:

1. Ask for references—employers, relatives, other churches who have dealt with the person—and contact them.

2. Pay the person's bill(s) directly to the creditor rather than handing the money to the individual.

3. Try for long-term solutions that include employment and help in money management instead of one-time handouts.

4. Don't hesitate to attach appropriate "strings" to financial aid, such as requiring counseling for a person whose emotional instability hampers the ability to keep a job. Don't use "strings" as a way to *avoid* helping the needy, however.

5. Don't let yourself be manipulated into giving against your better judgment. "Con artists" often know how to use your guilt or naiveté against you. If necessary, call another church leader into the situation or wait a day before deciding what to do.

6. Know when and where to refer cases you can't handle.

Slow Solutions. Observe that lasting solutions to financial crisis take time. When the victim's attitudes or beliefs are causing the problem, confrontation and discipline by church leaders may be necessary. Review your church's policies on corporate discipline. Then read II Thessalonians 3:6, 11-15. What attitude does Paul warn against? How is church discipline to be used in this situation? What is the ultimate aim of such discipline? How could accountability to a church leader help a person who misuses credit? How could it help one who has difficulty sticking to a budget? Discuss ways in which your church could use a combination of accountability, training, and financial aid to help victims of financial crisis.

SESSION 3: CAN WE DO MORE?

Aim: To brainstorm ways to better serve those in financial crisis, and to involve more members in this ministry.

The Unmet Needs. Read Matthew 25:31-46. What kinds of needy people does Christ call us to help in this passage? (The hungry, the thirsty, the strangers, those who need clothes, those who are sick, those in prison.) Which of these needs may be related to financial problems? (All could be; refugees could be "strangers," and sickness could result from inability to afford medical care.) Discuss what your church is doing to help people in these situations. Are present efforts adequate? Does the Matthew passage leave you feeling as though you need to do more?

Brainstorm. Without evaluating feasibility, list all the ways group members can think of to help those in financial crisis. Here are ideas to get you started: a telephone hot line for those who need financial advice; food pantry; "closet" of used clothing; assigning a church leader to help a member stick to a budget; job-hunting classes for the unemployed; a bulletinlike "need sheet" showing available jobs, available workers, requests for clothes or furniture, and other needs; appointing a person to coordinate responses to money problems; starting a fund to cover fees for those who can't afford camp or other church activities; taking youth and adult groups to pitch in at an inner-city mission; starting a day-care center, etc. After brainstorming, form action groups to discuss the ideas and commit themselves to following through on at least one idea per group.

Hidden Helpers. Use your church directory for reference as you consider ways to involve your congregation in helping the financially troubled. Do you have members (accountants, investors, bankers, etc.) who could advise nonsavers and debtors? Attorneys to help those who face bankruptcy or other money-related legal problems? Experienced householders who could help newlyweds and young singles set up and stick to a budget? People who could staff and solicit donations for a food pantry? Put suggestions in writing for follow-up by appropriate committees or individuals.

Additional Training Resources

You may find the following books useful as you raise awareness concerning financial needs in your church:

Building a Caring Church by Tom and Janie Lovorn (Victor Books, 1986). This how-to volume covers several aspects of caring ministry, with one chapter devoted specifically to meeting financial needs.

Healing the Wounded: The Costly Love of Church Discipline by John White and Ken Blue (InterVarsity Press, 1985). Some of the principles in this book could be adapted by church leaders who are ready to use loving confrontation to resolve attitude-based money problems.

Rich Christians in an Age of Hunger by Ronald J. Sider (InterVarsity Press, 1984 [revised edition]). This book details God's concern for the needy and calls the Church to help.

What'cha Gonna Do with What'cha Got? by Jim Jackson (David C. Cook, 1987). This course in "Christianomics" centers on learning to use money effectively and in a Christ-directed way. A 13-week study, it provides materials for adults, teens, and elementary children.

Your Money, Their Ministry: A Guide to Responsible Christian Giving by Edward J. Hales and J. Alan Youngren (Eerdmans, 1981). Principles for careful, effective giving—particularly to parachurch organizations—are included in this practical guide.

CHAPTER SEVEN

THE LAW:
WHERE TO FIND HELP

A BOOK ON MONEY WOULD NOT BE COMPLETE WITHOUT A look at the major laws that govern its use. Most of the law, however, is on the subject of credit or borrowing. And that's appropriate since most of the problems people have with money have something to do with credit.

Before looking at the laws that govern credit and borrowing money we should review the major types of lending programs or instruments that are available.

Charge Accounts[1]

Open or 30-day Account: This account is not as common as it was in the past, but is still used in some retail and department stores. If the account is not paid in the 30-day period, it may be carried over to the next month with a credit charge. The goods purchased on such accounts become the consumer's property immediately on delivery; they do not become subject to repossession should the customer fail to fulfill the legal and moral obligation to make payment.

Revolving Accounts: An open line of credit is established against which purchases are charged with monthly payments that include a service charge. The *optional* revolving account allows the customer to pay off the entire balance within 15 to 20 days without a charge.

Credit Cards: Limited Purpose Credit Cards—Issued by major companies like oil companies or department stores, these cards may only be used to purchase goods and services from the company that issued the card.

General Purpose Credit Cards—Issued by national firms for use in their own branches, but also accepted by other companies that are willing to bill and be paid by the card issuer. An airline credit card, for example, may be accepted by other airlines and some hotels. Often these are called "travel and entertainment" cards.

Bank Cards and Other Instruments—Sometimes called "redi-checks," "charge account banking," "privilege checking," or "checking plus," these are ways a bank gets in on the credit business.

Finance charges are usually calculated by dividing the sum of the balances outstanding for each day of the billing period by the number of days in the period, then multiplying by the daily rate of interest. The longer the payment is deferred, the higher are the resulting finance costs.

Installment Credit[2]

Installment credit is different from other forms of personal credit because it is amortized; that is, it is reduced by agreed upon weekly or monthly payments, each of which includes interest and retirement of some of the remaining principal.

Installment Sales or Loan Accounts: These accounts have many similarities: the frequency of payments (monthly, biweekly, or weekly installments) and the length (usually from 4 to 24 months but may be written for longer or shorter periods of time). The accounts are initiated by a written contract in which title to the articles purchased remains with the seller until the last payment is made, when it passes to the customer.

A Conditional Sales Contract: A contract like the installment sales or loan account described above. In addition to retaining title until the last payment is made, and repossessing the property in case of default, the seller may require the buyer to still pay the unpaid balance. Moreover, the seller does not have to repossess. Upon default, the whole unpaid balance may be declared to be due and the customer sued for this sum. Often, however, buyers are protected by a state law that requires the return to them of the excess of the merchandise's resale value over legal fees and reasonable financing costs, to the extent of the debtor's previous payments. Only when the whole unpaid balance has been liquidated is the buyer free from the contract.

A Bailment Lease: A contract that provides that the goods will be rented to the buyer, the "rent" being the agreed upon series of installment payments. Title is held by the seller during the period of credit extension. When the rent payments are completed, however, the seller agrees to turn the title over to the buyer for a nominal payment, such as one dollar. This form of contract is commonly used in the purchase of television sets.

A General Credit Contract: This is an installment buying contract, and has other names: a budget plan, a three-payment or six-payment plan, a revolving credit plan, an easy payment plan, a flexible account. In contrast to the other types of installment contracts that have been discussed, this contract does not give the seller the right to repossess. If the buyer defaults on payments, the seller has the right to sue.

Borrowing[3]

So far we've talked about buying on the installment plan or using credit cards. A person can also secure money by borrowing. In exploring the feasibility of applying for a cash loan, the methods of stating the loan charges should be scrutinized carefully, since factors such as credit standing, credit worthiness of the borrower, amount to be borrowed, type and length of loan, and other criteria will determine how much a person will pay for the use of the money.

There are three methods generally used to state finance charges:

1. The Add-on Method—Charge is calculated as if the borrower had the use of the total amount of the loan for the full period, and this charge is added to the amount of the loan. If payments are late, an additional charge may be incurred.

2. The Discount Method—Charge is calculated exactly like the add-on method except the finance charge is deducted from the face amount of the loan before the borrower receives it. For instance, on a note for $1500, discounted at 7 percent per year, the interest for 15 months would amount to $131.25. The borrower receives only $1368.75, because 7 percent is taken off at the outset. If the borrower had needed the full $1500, it would have been necessary to borrow enough to allow for the discounting.

3. The Simple Interest Method—The lender charges interest only on the exact amount borrowed for the exact amount of time it is loaned. This method has a built-in reward for early payment and a penalty for being late.

There are many types of organizations that lend money. Following is a brief description of the most common ones and some of the ways they do business:

Commercial Banks—Offer both commercial and personal loans. Commercial loans are for a short amount of time, usually

60 or 90 days, and the interest rate fluctuates with the general economic situation. These loans are secured by negotiable collateral. Personal loans are secured by personal property or by a note signed by one or more responsible endorsers. Most commercial banks use the advance discount rate of charging interest and many require credit life insurance. There may also be a fee for investigation of credit worthiness and a minimum service charge.

Savings and Loan Associations—Lend chiefly to finance the purchase or construction of homes, farms, or other real estate, or to remodel, repair, or improve property. In most states they restrict themselves to mortgage loans, but in some they also lend money for general purposes.

Consumer Finance and Small Loan Companies—Governed by state licensing and by legal limits on interest rates and size of loans. Rates for cash loans vary from 36 percent annually on the smallest to 12 percent on larger, well-secured loans. While the average is about 21 percent, interest in some states can go as high as 42 percent. Loans can usually be secured without verified evidence regarding assets that reduce and liabilities that add to the risk of making the loan. Loans are usually paid in regular installments within 20 months.

Credit Unions—Consumer cooperative lending agencies chartered by the state or federal government to make loans to members of the cooperative at a low annual percentage rate. They make small loans and finance such things as automobiles and durable goods. Most of the credit unions' business is conducted by employees of large business firms, governmental organizations, or churches.

Credit unions usually charge a legal maximum of 1 percent per month on the unpaid balance, although in a few places the rate is .8 percent. The maximum loan period is for two years. On loans $50 and the usual maximum of $500 the endorsement of a responsible endorser is required, unless the borrower can pledge shares equal in value. Many credit unions insist on wage assignments which allow the union to deduct loan payments from salaries of delinquent borrowers without court hearings.

The Pawnbroker—Primary source of credit for the nearly destitute person whose creditworthiness has not or cannot be established. Pawnbrokers are licensed, state regulated, and usually required to execute and file a bond. Although they charge a high interest rate, they provide the quickest form of loan service.

Loans are made only on pledges, usually personal goods, tools, jewelry, etc.

The pawnbroker is subject to taxes and must generally keep records of pledges. Permissible interest rates in some states may be up to 3.5 percent per month and in others up to 5 percent per month for certain amounts, the interest decreasing on loans for greater amounts. In some states a service charge is allowed. In effect, pawnbroker rates range from 24 percent to 120 percent a year.

Ordinarily a pawnbroker will lend only from 60 percent to 90 percent of the auction value of the asset that has been pledged against the loan, and the asset must be left with the pawnbroker for the life of the loan. The borrower is given a pawn ticket showing the date, the amount of the loan, description of the property pledged, and sometimes the monthly interest rate and maturity of the loan. The pledge usually can be redeemed within a year by payment of the loan and the interest due. The loan must be repaid in a lump sum. If the loan is not repaid within the specified period, the lender has the right to sell the pledge, ordinarily at public auction.

Veterans' Loans—Available to veterans with honorable discharges after at least 90 days of active service (or fewer if there is a service connected disability). These loans are available for a variety of purposes, even buying a business or liquidating delinquent indebtedness incurred in connection with these enterprises. Second-mortgage loans may also be secured although the costs of such loans often involve exorbitant handling fees. Interest on a second mortgage may be as high as 15 percent.

Consumer Protection[4]

The Consumer Credit Protection Act of 1968, which launched Truth in Lending, was a landmark piece of legislation. For the first time, creditors were required to state the cost of borrowing in a common language so that the consumer could figure out exactly what charges would be, compare costs, and shop for credit.

Since 1968, credit protections have multiplied rapidly. The concepts of "fair" and "equal" credit have been written into laws that outlaw discrimination in credit transactions, require that consumers be told the reason when credit is denied, give borrowers access to their credit records, and set up a method to settle billing disputes.

Information Pertaining to the Cost of Credit. Two laws apply in this area:

Truth in Lending: Requires creditors to give you certain basic information about the cost of buying on credit or taking out a loan. These disclosures can help you shop around for the best deal.

Truth in Leasing: Disclosures can help you compare the cost and terms of one lease with another and with the cost and terms of buying for cash or on credit.

There are several things you should understand about the cost of credit. The first is the finance charge and the second is the annual percentage rate. Under Truth in Lending, the creditor must tell you in writing before you sign what the finance charge and annual percentage rate will be for the amount of money borrowed.

The finance charge is the total dollar amount you pay to use credit. It includes interest costs, and sometimes other costs, such as service charges and some credit-related insurance premiums or appraisal fees. You should remember, it includes all costs to use credit.

The annual percentage rate (APR) is the percentage cost (or relative cost) of credit on a yearly basis. This is your key to comparing costs, regardless of the amount of credit or how long you have to repay it.

Cost of Open-end Credit: Open-end credit includes credit cards, department store cards, and check-overdraft accounts that allow you to write checks for more than your actual balance. Open-end credit can be used again and again, generally until you reach a certain prearranged borrowing limit. Before the person signs the agreement, any institution that extends open-end credit by law must:

1. State the cost of credit in terms of the finance charge and the APR.

2. Tell the person the method of calculating the finance charge.

3. Tell the person when the finance charges begin.

Leasing Costs and Terms: Leasing gives a person temporary use of property in return for periodic payments. The Truth in Leasing Law requires the leasing company to:

1. Give the person a written statement of costs, including the amount of any security deposit, the amount of monthly payments, and the amount that must be paid for license, registration, taxes, and maintenance.

2. Give the person a written statement about terms, including any insurance needed, guarantees, information about who is responsible for servicing the property, any standards for its wear and tear, and whether or not the person has the option to buy the property.

Open-end Leases and Balloon Payments: The costs for this type of lease will depend on whether the person chooses an "open-end" lease or a "closed-end" lease. Open-end leases usually offer lower monthly payments than closed-end leases, but the person may owe a large extra payment, often called a "balloon" payment, based on the value of the property when it is returned.

For instance, suppose you lease a car under a three-year open-end lease. The leasing company estimates the car will be worth $4000 after three years of normal use. If you bring back the car in a condition that makes it worth only $3500, you may owe a balloon payment of $500.

Closed-end leases usually have a higher monthly payment than open-end leases, but there is no balloon payment at the end of the lease.

The leasing company must:

1. Tell the person whether he or she owes a balloon payment and how it will be calculated.

2. Give the person, at his or her expense, the right to an independent appraisal of the property's worth at the end of the lease.

3. Limit (usually) a balloon payment to no more than three times the average monthly payment.

Advertising: Both Truth in Lending and Truth in Leasing require accurate advertising of terms. These laws say that if a business mentions one important feature of a credit sale, loan, open-end credit plan, or lease, such as the down payment, it must also state other important features, such as the annual percentage rate and the terms of repayment. An ad must also specify if a leasing arrangement is involved.

Costs of Settlement on a House: A house is probably the single largest credit purchase for most consumers, and one of the most complicated. The Real Estate Settlement Procedures Act, like Truth in Lending, is a disclosure law. The act, administered by the Department of Housing and Urban Development, requires the lender to give the person, in advance, certain information about the costs that will have to be paid when the person actually gets the deed to the property. This event is called settlement, and the law helps the person shop for low settlement costs. To find out more about this subject write to:

Assistant Secretary of Consumer Affairs and Regulatory Functions
Attention: RESPA Office, US/HUD
451 7th Street SW, Room 9266
Washington, DC 20410

Information Related to Applying for Credit: One law applies to this area.

The Equal Credit Opportunity Act: This law starts all credit applicants off on the same footing. It says that race, color, age, sex, marital status, and certain other factors may not be used to discriminate against a person in any part of a credit dealing.

When a creditor is reviewing the credit application of a person he or she is looking for three things:

1. Capacity: Can the person repay the loan?

2. Character: Will the person repay the loan? What kind of history of payment does the person have?

3. Collateral: Is the creditor protected if the person fails to pay? Creditors want to know what a person has to secure the loan.

The Equal Credit Opportunity Act does not guarantee that the person will get credit. Each must still pass the creditor's tests of creditworthiness. But the creditor must apply these tests fairly. The creditor may not deny a person credit because of age, sex, marital status, race, color, religion, national origin, because the person exercises his or her rights under Federal credit laws. A creditor may not use any of these grounds as an excuse to discourage a person from applying for a loan; refuse a person a loan if he or she qualifies; lend a person money on terms different from those granted another person with similar income, expenses, credit history, and collateral.

There are special rules that spell out the law in more detail in the following areas:

Age—Older persons may not be discriminated against because of age although the law permits a creditor to consider certain information related to it, such as how long until the person retires, or how long the income will continue.

Public Assistance—A creditor can consider how old the person's dependents are or whether the person will continue to meet the residency requirements for receiving benefits, but may not deny credit because the person is receiving public assistance.

Housing Loans—In addition to banning discrimination because of the applicant's race, color, sex, religion, etc., the law prohibits creditors from discriminating because of the race or national origin of the people in the neighborhood where the person wants to live or buy a house, and from using any appraisal of the value of the property that considers the race of the people in the neighborhood.

Discrimination Against Women—A creditor may not:

1. Ask for the person's sex on the application form except on a loan to buy or build a home.

2. Ask a woman about her child-bearing plans.

3. Ask the person to disclose child support or alimony payments, although if the person does the creditor must count them.

4. Ask if a woman has a telephone listing her name.

5. Refuse to open an account just because of sex or marital status. A woman may choose to use her first name and maiden name, her first name and her husband's last name, or a combined last name. If a woman is creditworthy a creditor may not require the husband to cosign the account except when property rights are involved. Creditors may not ask for information about husbands or ex-husbands, unless the income received is alimony, child support, or separate maintenance payments.

6. Require a woman to reapply for credit just because she has married, been divorced, or become widowed. Nor may creditors close accounts for these reasons. There must be some sign that the woman's creditworthiness has changed. For example, creditors may ask a woman to reapply if she relied on the ex-husband's income to get credit in the first place.

A person must be notified within 30 days after an application has been properly completed and turned in whether the application has been approved. If credit is denied, the notice must be in writing and it must explain the specific reasons for denying credit or tell the person his or her right to request an explanation. The person has the same rights if an account is closed.

If a person thinks he or she has been discriminated against, the person should cite the law to the lender. If the lender does not provide a satisfactory answer, the person should contact a federal enforcement agency listed later in this chapter.

Information Related to Credit Histories and Records: Two laws apply in this area.

The Equal Credit Opportunity Act: Gives people a way to establish credit history and identity.

The Fair Credit Reporting Act: Sets up a procedure for correcting mistakes on a person's credit record.

Mistakes on a person's credit record, sometimes mistaken identities, can cloud a person's credit future. The Fair Credit Reporting Act states that a person may examine information in his or her credit file and have any errors corrected. This information falls in three categories:

1. Negative Information: If a lender refuses a person credit because of unfavorable information on a credit report, the person has the right to the name and address of the agency that keeps the report. The information may be requested either by mail or in person. Usually the person will not get an exact copy of the file, just a summary of the information in it. The law states that the agency must help the person interpret the data, because it's raw data that takes experience to analyze. If a person challenges a credit refusal within 30 days of the time of refusal, the agency may not charge a fee for giving the information.

The agency or credit bureau will remove from a person's record any errors the creditor admits are there. If the person disagrees with the findings, he or she can file a short statement in the record giving his or her side of the story. Future reports to creditors must include this statement or a summary of it.

2. Old Information—Sometimes credit information is too old to give a good picture of a person's financial reputation. There is a limit on how long certain kinds of information may be kept in a person's file. Bankruptcies must usually be removed from a person's credit history after ten years. Suits and judgments, tax liens, arrest records, and most other kinds of unfavorable information must usually be removed after seven years.

3. Billing Mistakes—This is covered in the next section.

Information Related to Correcting Credit Mistakes: Two laws apply in this area:

1. The Fair Credit Billing Act sets up a procedure for promptly correcting billing mistakes, for refusing to make credit card payments on defective goods, and for promptly crediting payments.

2. Truth in Lending gives a person three days to change his or her mind about certain mortgage contracts. It also limits a person's risk on lost or stolen credit cards.

The Fair Credit Billing Act requires creditors to correct errors promptly and without damage to a person's credit rating. The law defines a billing error as any charge for something the person didn't buy or for a purchase made by someone not authorized to use the account; that is not properly identified on the person's bill or is for an amount different from the actual purchase price or was entered on a date different from the purchase date; for something that the person did not accept on delivery or that was not delivered according to agreement.

Billing errors also include: errors in arithmetic; failure to reflect a payment or other credit to the person's account; failure to mail the statement to the person's current address, provided the person notified the creditor of an address change at least 20 days before the end of the billing period; a questionable item, or an item for which the person needs additional information.

If there is an error on a bill, there are specific steps people should take to correct it. They should:
1. Notify the creditor in writing within 60 days after the bill was mailed. The creditor should be told: the person's name; that there is an error and why the person believes there is; the suspected amount of the error or the item the person wants explained.
2. Pay all parts of the bill that are not in dispute. While waiting for a settlement, the person does not have to pay the disputed amount or any charge related to it.

The creditor must acknowledge the person's letter within 30 days, unless the problem can be resolved in that time. Within two billing periods, but in no case longer than 90 days, either the person's account must be corrected or the creditor must tell the person why he or she believes the bill is correct. If the creditor is right, the person must pay all past due amounts plus any finance charges assigned to those amounts during the dispute period.

The Fair Credit Billing Act also states that a creditor may not threaten a person's credit rating while the person is resolving a billing dispute. A person may withhold payment on any damaged or poor-quality services purchased with a credit card, as long as the person has made a real attempt to solve the problem. This right may be limited if the card was not issued by the store where the purchase was made. In such cases, the sale must have been for more than $50, and must have taken place in the person's home state or within 100 miles of the person's address. A creditor must bill and credit the person's payments promptly. A person may change his or her mind on any transaction in which the person has used a home as security to get credit. A person has three business days to think about the transaction and to cancel it if desired. The creditor must give the person a written notice of the right to cancel and the person must notify the creditor in writing of the desire to cancel. If a person is in a hurry and needs credit immediately he or she may give up the right to cancel by providing a written explanation of the circumstances. This right to cancel was provided to protect individuals against hasty decisions that might endanger the continued home ownership. This law does not apply to home mortgages.

If a credit card is stolen, a person must notify the card company. The most a person will have to pay for unauthorized charges is $50 on each card, even if someone runs up several hundred dollars on the stolen card. (It is illegal for a card issuer to send a person a card unless the card has been requested. However, a card issuer may send the person a new card to replace an expired one, without the person's request.)

Information Related to Electronic Fund Transfers: One law applies in this area. The Electronic Fund Transfer Act assures the person that the electronic transaction can be documented in printed/paper form.

If a person uses a cash machine he or she can get a written receipt showing the amount of the transfer, the date it was made, and other information. A bank statement must also show all electronic transfers to and from the account, including those made at electronic terminals, or by a preauthorized arrangement, or under a telephone transfer plan. It will also name the party to whom payment has been made and show any fee for the EFT services.

If there has been an error in an electronic fund transfer:

1. The person must write or call the institution no later than 60 days from the time the first statement containing the alleged error was mailed.

2. The institution must promptly investigate the error and resolve it within 45 days. However, if the institution takes longer than ten business days to complete its investigation, generally it must recredit the person's account for the amount in question while it finishes the investigation.

3. The institution must notify the person of the results of its investigation. If there was an error, the institution must correct it promptly. If it finds no error, the institution must explain in writing why it believes there was no error. The person may ask for copies of documents relied on for the investigation.

If an EFT card is lost or stolen, the liability for an unauthorized withdrawal is limited to $50, if the person notifies the financial institution within two business days after learning of the loss or theft of the card or code. But, people could lose as much as $500 if they do not tell the card issuer within two business days after learning of the loss or theft.

If the person does not report an unauthorized transfer that appears on his or her statement within 60 days after the statement has been mailed, the person risks unlimited loss on transfers made after the 60-day period. This means that a person could lose all the money in the account plus the maximum overdraft line of credit.

Complaints[5]

Even in today's complex marketplace, a person should expect quality products and services at a fair price. The following steps should be taken when something goes wrong.

1. *Identify the Problem.* What must be done to resolve it? Do you want your money back, the product repaired, or will an exchange do?

2. *Gather Documentation.* Get sales receipts, repair orders, warranties, canceled checks, or contracts to back up your complaint.

3. *Go Back to Where You Made the Purchase.* Contact the person who sold you the item or performed the service. Calmly and accurately explain the problem and what action you would like taken. If the person is not helpful, ask for a supervisor and repeat your complaint. Allow each person a reasonable period of time to resolve the problem before contacting the next person.

4. *Don't Give Up.* If you are not satisfied and the company operates nationally, write the person responsible for consumer complaints at the headquarters office. If the company doesn't have a consumer office, write the president of the company.

5. *Where to Write.* If you can't find who to write, either through the information on your documentation or in the phone book, go to the library and look through Standard & Poor's Register of Corporations, Directors, and Executives. It lists over 45,000 American business firms. If you don't have the name of the manufacturer of the product, check your local library for the Thomas Register. It lists the manufacturers of thousands of products.

6. *What to Write.* Include your name, address, home and work phone. Type the letter if possible. If handwritten, make sure it is easy to read.

Make the letter brief. Include all the facts like where you bought the item, the date of purchase, and any information about the product or service, such as serial and model numbers or specific type of service.

State exactly what you want done.

Include copies of all documents. Not originals.

Avoid writing angry, sarcastic, or threatening letters. The person reading the letter was not responsible for the problem. Be reasonable.

Keep a copy of the letter for your records.

For complaints about lawyers, write the American Bar Association at the national headquarters, 750 North Lake Shore Drive, Chicago, IL 60611.

For complaints about financial planners write The International Association of Financial Planning, 2 Concourse Parkway, Suite 800, Atlanta, GA 30328, or the Institute of Certified Financial Planners at 3443 South Galena, Suite 190, Denver, CO 80231-5093.

For complaints about tax preparers, contact the Internal Revenue Service. If the tax preparer is a certified public accountant, you could contact the state board of certified public accountants.

For complaints about real estate brokers and agents, contact the state licensing or regulatory agency. This is usually the Real Estate Commission or the Department or Division of Real Estate. Complaints can also be directed to the National Association of Realtors, 777 14th Street, NW, Washington, DC 20005.

Sources of Help

If you have failed in your attempt to get your complaint resolved directly with the person or company you did business with, there are other sources of help.

For Industry Consumer Complaints—Go to your local library

and check in the directory entitled National Trade & Professional Associations of The U.S. and Canada and Labor Unions.

For General Help with Business—The Better Business Bureaus (BBB) are nonprofit organizations sponsored by private, local businesses. Look in the phone book for one in your area. And if you can't find one, write the national office at 1515 Wilson Boulevard, Arlington, VA 22209. The BBB offer a wide range of services related to business.

Using the Media for Help—Local newspapers and radio-TV stations offer "Action" or "Hotline" services where consumers with problems can get help. Check your local phone book, newspapers, or library for how to contact them.

State, County and City Consumer Offices—If you are not satisfied with a company's response you may direct your complaint to a local or state consumer office. Look in your phone book under city, county, and state government listings.

Federal Agencies—Some Federal agencies have enforcement responsibilities for specific consumer problems. Others take action for the benefit of the public as a whole. Check your phone book for listings under "Federal Information Center" and call them. They will direct you to the office that may help you. If you can't find a listing in your city, check your state capitol or look through Federal directories in your library.

Small Claims Courts—If you have a complaint that you have not been able to resolve, you may want to go to small claims court. Court procedures are generally simple, inexpensive, quick, and informal. Court fees are nominal, and you often get your filing fee back if you win your case. Generally, you won't need a lawyer. In fact, in some states, lawyers are not permitted. These courts, as the name suggests, are for small claims. The maximum amounts that can be claimed or awarded differ from state. Look in your phone book under *government* for small claims court listings.

Legal Aid and Legal Services—Legal Aid and Legal Services offices help people who cannot afford to hire private lawyers, and who meet financial eligibility requirements. There are more than 1000 of these offices around the country. All offer free legal services to those who qualify. Look in your phone book under "Legal" or "Legal Services" or "Attorney."

Private Lawyers—If you need a lawyer, check with the Lawyer Referral Service of your state, city, or county bar association. Local and state bar associations are usually listed in the area telephone directories. If you have a complaint about a lawyer, contact the American Bar Association at its national headquarters: 750 North Lake Shore Drive, Chicago, IL 60611.

Private and Voluntary Consumer Groups—These groups are usually created to advocate various and specific consumer interests. In some communities they help individual consumers with their complaints. To find out if such a group exists in your community, contact your state or local consumer affairs office.

Consumer Credit Counseling Services—Counseling services provide aid to individuals having difficulty budgeting their money and/or meeting necessary monthly expenses. Many organizations, including credit unions, family service centers and religious organizations offer some type of credit counseling. Another source of help is the Consumer Credit Counseling Services (CCCS), sponsored by the National Foundation of Consumer Credit. The CCCS counseling program provides money management techniques, debt payment plans, and educational programs. The CCCS has affiliated agencies in over 250 cities in the country. Look in your local phone directory or contact the National Foundation for Consumer Credit, 8701 Georgia Avenue, Suite 601, Silver Spring, MD 20910.

Family Service America—The FSA is a national nonprofit membership organization supporting a network of approximately 290 local family service agencies. FSA works to make families healthy by helping them build stronger relationships, make positive adjustments to life changes, understand the pressures of today's living, and create contentment at home and on the job. FSA provides a full range of counseling, including financial. For an office near you, contact FSA at 11700 West Lake Park Drive, Park Place, Milwaukee, WI 53224.

Other Consumer Information—The Federal Government offers more than 200 free or low-cost booklets on a variety of topics. Many would be helpful in addressing consumer complaints or problems. The topics are listed in the Consumer Information Catalog offered free by the Consumer Information Center, Pueblo, CO 81009.

Chapter One

1. *The 1986 Information Please Almanac* (Houghton Mifflin Company, New York, 1985), p. 61.
2. Arnold Mitchell, *The Nine American Lifestyles* (Macmillan Publishing Co., New York, 1983), cover.
3. Ibid, p. 3.
4. Ibid, p. vii.
5. U.S. Bureau of the Census, *Statistical Abstract of the United States: 1986*, 106th edition, (Washington, DC, 1985), p. 502.
6. Eric Gelman with Rich Thomas and Carolyn Friday, *Is Consumer Debt Too High?* (Newsweek, December 23, 1985), p. 55.
7. U.S. Bureau of the Census, *Statistical Abstract of the United States: 1986*, 106th edition, (Washington, DC, 1985), derived from statistics on pages 501 & 502.
8. Ibid, p. 502.
9. *Chicago Tribune,* November 9, 1986, p. 31.
10. U.S. Bureau of the Census, *Statistical Abstract of the United States: 1986*, 106th edition, (Washington, DC, 1985), p. 502.
11. Ibid, p. 501.
12. Ibid, p. 502.
13. Reader's Digest Association, Inc., *Reader's Digest 1986 Almanac and Yearbook* (Pleasantville, New York, 1985), p. 737.

Chapter Three

1. Susan Jacoby, *Compulsive Shopping*, (Glamour Magazine: April 1986), p. 319.
2. Ibid, p. 349.
3. Ibid, p. 350.
4. U.S. Bureau of the Census, *Statistical Abstract of the United*

States: 1986, 106th edition, (Washington, DC, 1985), p. 522.
5. Managing Your Credit (Household Finance Corporation, Prospect Heights, Illinois, 1978), p. 33.
6. Mary-Margaret Wantuck, *A Better Balance in Bankruptcy Law* (Nations Business: April, 1985), p. 51.
7. Ibid, p. 51.
8. Richard Bolles, *What Color Is Your Parachute?* (Ten Speed Press, Berkeley, 1984), p. 68.
9. Ibid, p. 75.
10. Ibid, pp. 104, 105.
11. Ibid, pp. 109, 110.
12. ibid, pp. 114, 115.

Chapter Four
1. Richard Foster, *Money, Sex, and Power* (Harper & Row, San Francisco 1985), p. 74.
2. Ibid, p. 29.

Chapter Five
1. Richard Foster, *Money, Sex, and Power* (Harper & Row, San Francisco, 1985), p. 72.

Chapter Seven
1. Frances Lomas Feldman, *The Family in Today's Money World,* (Family Service America, 1976), pp. 324-329. This book may be ordered for $13.95 (cloth), $10 (paperback), plus $2 for shipping, from FSA, 11700 West Lake Park Drive, Park Place, Milwaukee, WI 53224. Family Service America is a national nonprofit membership organization supporting a network of approximately 290 local family service agencies. It can direct you to a member agency in your city that offers a wide range of family counseling including help with finances and career.
2. Ibid, pp. 330-334.
3. Ibid, pp. 334-344.
4. Federal Reserve System, *Consumer Handbook to Credit Protection Laws*, 6th printing (Washington, DC, 1983), pp. 1-37.
5. United States Office of Consumer Affairs, *Consumer's Resource Handbook* (Washington, DC, January 1986 edition), pp. 1-6.

RESOURCES FOR HELPING

Financial

Bowman, George, M., 1979. *How to Succeed with Your Money*. Chicago, Ill.: Moody Press. A plan for money management with special emphasis on Christian stewardship.

Burkett, Larry, 1985. *Teaching Your Children About Money*. Waco, Texas: Life-Liter Cassette of Word Publishing. This cassette is an excellent resource for teaching children about money. Mr. Burkett asserts that teaching children in their early years will prevent financial problems in adulthood.

Burkett, Larry, 1982. *Your Finances in Changing Times*. Chicago, Ill.: Moody Press. A look at how the economy works, God's principles of finance, and God's plan for your financial management.

Dayton, Howard, Jr., 1979. *Your Money: Frustration or Freedom*. Wheaton, Ill.: Tyndale House Publishers. Financial planning from a Biblical perspective. Dayton asserts that if you follow his suggestions, tensions related to money will disappear.

Hill, Harold, 1984. *The Money Book for King's Kids*. Old Tappan, N.J.: Fleming H. Revell. Another view on finances and Biblical wisdom as it relates to prosperity.

Johnson, Albert. J., 1983. *A Christian Guide to Family Finances*. Wheaton, Ill.: Victor Books. A Bible-based book that helps the Christian work through money problems. Covers money management, borrowing, lending, bankruptcy, credit, wills, and much more.

Ludwig, Thomas; Westphal, Merold; Klay, Robin; and Myers, David, 1981. *Inflation, Poortalk, and the Gospel*. Valley Forge, Pa.: Judson Press. Guidance to help Christians respond to today's economy in ways that are Biblically sound and practical.

MacArthur, Dr. John. *You, Your Money, and God's Plan*. Ventura, Ca: Listen and Grow Tapes of Gospel Light Publications. An audio cassette study that focuses on the Christian and finances.

MacGregor, Malcolm, 1977. *Financial Planning Guide for Your Money Matters*. Minneapolis, Minn.: Bethany House Publishers. The companion to *Your Money Matters* with work sheets for financial planning.

MacGregor, Malcolm, 1977. *Your Money Matters*. Minneapolis, Minn.: Bethany House Publishers. Bible-centered guidebook covering everything about the subject of money and the Christian life. Written by a CPA.

Murray, Andrew, 1978. *Money, Christ's Perspective on the Use and Abuse of Money*. Minneapolis, Minn.: Bethany House Publishers. Practical how-to book that helps a Christian acquire the right attitude about possessions.

Rusford, Patricia, 1984. *From Money Mess to Money Management*. Old Tappan, N.J.: Fleming H. Revell. A guide to personal finance for Christian women.

Schuller, Robert, 1984. *The Power of Being Debt Free*. Nashville, Tenn.: Thomas Nelson, Inc., Publishers. How eliminating the national debt could improve your standard of living.

Schweyer, Ruth Ann. *Family Financial Planning*. Minneapolis, Minn.: Augsburg Press. 16-page handbook designed to help families evaluate their financial situation and make decisions. Includes family exercises.

Sproul, R. C., Jr., 1985. *Money Matters*. Wheaton, Ill.: Tyndale House Publishers. Offers original insights about inflation, profit, taxation, materialism, etc. A new conservative look at money and personal finances.

Wilson, Ken, 1983. *Your Money and Your Life*. Ann Arbor, Mich.: Servant Publications. A practical guide for earning, managing, and giving your money.

Christian Living

Balchin, John, 1985. *Citizens of Another Kingdom*. Colorado Springs, Co.: Navpress. Helps Christians adopt God's values while recognizing the influence and pressure of earthly values.

Briscoe, Stuart D.,1985. *Practical Wisdom from the Bible*. Old Tappan, N.J.: Fleming H. Revell. Practical advice for successful Christian living. Topics like accumulation of wealth, control of emotions, and behavior.

Collins, Gary R., 1983. *Calm Down*. Ventura, Ca.: Vision House Books of Gospel Light Publications. Noted Christian psychologist offers hope and help to everyone who struggles with everyday living.

Foster, Richard, 1985. *Money, Sex, and Power*. San Francisco, Ca.: Harper and Row. A powerful look at three major forces in our lives and how to control them as Christians.

Galloway, Dale E., 1983. *Dare to Discipline Yourself*. Old Tappan, N.J.: Fleming H. Revell. Easy-to-practice guidelines for achieving discipline in all areas of life.

LaHaye, Tim, 1983. *The Battle for the Family*. Old Tappan, N.J.: Fleming H. Revell. The author identifies 15 humanistic forces that threaten the home and offers practical advice to help Christians battle against them.

MacArthur, John, Jr., 1986. *Overcoming Materialism*. Chicago, Ill.: Moody Press. A book that helps evaluate motives, attitudes, and thought patterns. Aim: to make God the center of your life.

MacDonald, Gordon, 1986. *Ordering Your Private World*. Nashville, Tenn.: Thomas Nelson, Inc., Publishers. Explains how by nurturing our inner life we can learn to reappraise our frantic life-styles and bring order and peace.

Ross, Lanson, 1982. *Total Life Prosperity*. Wheaton, Ill.: Tyndale House Publishers. A fresh look at how God characterizes a prospering person: having self-esteem, being goal oriented, budgeting and controlling finances, handling crisis, etc.

Taylor, Richard S., 1974. *The Disciplined Life*. Minneapolis, Minn.: Bethany House Publishers. A classic on the theme of a well-ordered Christian life.

Taylor, Richard S., 1975. *The Disciplined Lifestyle*. Minneapolis, Minn.: Bethany House Publishers. An appeal for a lifestyle that is consistent with both New Testament ethics and the standards of excellence in our society.

Vogt, Virgil, 1982. *Treasure in Heaven*. Ann Arbor, Mich.: Servant Publications. A challenge to bring our finances into line with God's Word.

Yohn, Rick, 1985. *Overcoming*. Colorado Springs, Co.: Navpress. A Bible study that deals with discouragement, covetousness, misfortune, handicaps, selfishness and ways to deal with them.

Counseling

Adams, Jay E., 1986. *The Jay Adams Library of Christian Counseling*. Grand Rapids, Mich.: Ministry Resource Library of

Zondervan Publishing House. An excellent 16-book set for all types of Christian counseling situations.

Carter, Leslie, 1986. *Mind Over Emotions*. Waco, Tx: Word Publishing. Helps Christians understand how emotions drive behavior and what to do about it.

Collins, Gary R., 1986. *Innovative Approaches to Counseling*. Waco Tx.: Word Publishing. Excellent handbook on Christian counseling with special emphasis on community and service.

Feldman, Frances Lomas, 1976. *The Family in Today's Money World*. Milwaukee, Wis.: FSA. Available from FSA, 11700 West Lake Park Dr., Milwaukee, Wisconsin 53224. Complete guide to counseling families in financial crisis.

Kelfer, Russell, 1985. *Self-Control*. Wheaton, Ill.: Tyndale House Publishers. Thirteen-week adult elective that helps Christians gain control of their lives.

Sehnert, Keith W., M.D., 1981. *Stress/Unstress*. Minneapolis, Minn.: Augsburg Press. Helps Christians move out of stressful situations. Includes Personal Action Plan to implement unstress techniques.

Wright, H. Norman, 1986. *How to Have a Creative Crisis*. Waco, Tx.: Word Publishing. How crisis points can be transformed into turning points. Helpful for counselors and pastors or anyone helping others in crisis situations.

Practical Help

Money Management Booklet Library, available from HFC, 2700 Sanders Road, Prospect Heights, Illinois 60070. For $5.00 you receive 12 booklets ranging in topics from financial planning, credit, shopping, children's spending, saving, investing, etc.

Career

Bolles, Richard, 1984. *What Color Is Your Parachute?* Berkeley, Ca.: Ten Speed Press. Excellent and complete guide to career planning. A must for every counselor's library.

Bramlett, James, 1986. *Work, A Handbook*. Grand Rapids, Mich.: Pyranne Books of Zondervan Publishing. Practical Christian guide to help in career planning: analyze the job market, use of placement organizations, preparation of a resume, how to be interviewed, etc.

Giving

MacArthur, John F., Jr., 1979. *Giving: God's Way.* Wheaton, Ill.: Tyndale House Publishers. An exploration of God's unchanging stand in financial matters. Principles from the Old and New Testament.

Martin, Dr. Walter. *Tithing.* Ventura, Ca.: Listen and Grow Tapes of Gospel Light Publications. Audio cassette on the principles of tithing.

Stafford, Bill, 1976. *The Adventure of Giving.* Wheaton, Ill.: Tyndale House Publishers. A practical guide to Christian giving.

Retirement—Estate Planning

Nauheim, Fred, 1982. *The Retirement Money Book.* New York: Acropolis Books. Excellent and complete book for retirement planning available at your local bookstore or public library.

Soled, Alex J. *The Essential Guide to Wills, Estates, Trusts, and Death Taxes.* American Association of Retired Persons (AARP) Books, 400 South Edward Street, Mount Prospect, Ill. 60056.

Watts, John, 1980. *Leave Your House in Order.* Wheaton, Ill.: Tyndale House Publishers. A book that helps Christians make orderly and God-honoring arrangements of financial affairs in provision for those left behind after death.

Booklets/Pamphlets

A Guide to Understanding Your Pension Plan. Send $3.00 to the Pension Rights Center, 1346 Connecticut Ave., NW, Washington, DC 20036.

Planning Retirement Income, Public Affairs Pamphlet No. 634. Available for $1.00 from Public Affairs Pamphlets, 381 Park Ave. South, New York, NY 10016.

Tax Benefits for Older Americans. IRS Publication No. 554 available free from your local IRS office.